MILL'S *UTILITARIANISM*

Continuum Reader's Guides

Aristotle's Nicomachean Ethics – Christopher Warne

Hegel's Philosophy of Right – David Rose

Heidegger's Being and Time – William Blattner

Hobbes's Leviathan – Laurie Bagby

Hume's Enquiry Concerning Human Understanding – Alan Bailey and Dan O'Brian

Hume's Dialogues Concerning Natural Religion – Andrew Pyle

Kant's Critique of Pure Reason – James Luchte

Kant's Groundwork for the Metaphysics of Morals – Paul Guyer

Locke's Essay Concerning Human Understanding – William Uzgalis

Mill's On Liberty – Geoffrey Scarre

Nietzsche's On the Genealogy of Morals – Daniel Conway

Plato's Republic – Luke Purshouse

Wittgenstein's Tractatus Logico-Philosophicus – Roger M. White

MILL'S *UTILITARIANISM*
A Reader's Guide

HENRY R. WEST

continuum

Continuum
The Tower Building
11 York Road
London SE1 7NX

80 Maiden Lane
Suite 704
New York NY 10038

www.continuumbooks.com

British Library Cataloguing-in-Publication Data
A catalogue record for this book is available from the British Library.

ISBN: HB: 0826493017
9780826493019
PB: 0826493025
9780826493026

Library of Congress Cataloging-in-Publication Data
A catalog record for this book is available from the Library of Congress.

Typeset by YHT Ltd, London
Printed and bound in Great Britain by
Cromwell Press, Trowbridge, Wiltshire

CONTENTS

Introduction   1

1. Context   3
   Alternatives to Utilitarianism   3
   Mill's Life and Writings   12
   Bentham's Utilitarian Philosophy   18

2. Overview of Themes   23

3. Reading the Text   28
   Overview: Subject Matter of the Chapters   28
   Chapter 1   29
   Chapter 2   38
   Chapter 3   69
   Chapter 4   77
   Chapter 5   89
   Summary   123

4. Reception and Influence   125

5. Notes for Further Reading   131
   Secondary Material   131
   Selective Bibliography   133

Index   137

INTRODUCTION

Utilitarianism is a position in philosophy that actions, laws and social policies are to be justified by their utility – that is, by their consequences. In 'classical' utilitarianism, as formulated by Jeremy Bentham (1748–1832) and John Stuart Mill (1806–73), the consequences that count are happiness and unhappiness. As Mill states the position, 'The creed which accepts as the foundation of morals, Utility, or the Greatest Happiness Principle, holds that actions are right in proportion as they tend to promote happiness, wrong as they tend to produce the reverse of happiness' (Mill 1861a: 210 [II, 2]); (references are to page numbers in *Collected Works of John Stuart Mill*, vol. 10, and to the chapter and paragraph of the work. References to this work will eliminate the author and year and simply have page numbers followed in brackets by chapter and paragraph. There are many reprints of the work, so chapter and paragraph are useful in looking up a citation in a reprint). It is a normative theory; it is a theory about what actions ought and ought not to be performed, what laws ought and ought not to be enacted and enforced, what policies ought and ought not to be adopted and carried out. Sometimes utility is part of an account of what people *in fact* are motivated to do and how they *in fact* justify their actions, but the importance of utilitarianism in recent philosophy is as a normative theory, a theory used to justify or to criticize existing practice and to recommend reform or radical change.

John Stuart Mill was the foremost British philosopher of the nineteenth century, recognized for his contributions in nearly all fields of philosophy. His essay *Utilitarianism* is the most widely read statement and defence of the utilitarian philosophy. It is therefore worthy of careful study. Mill's version of utilitarianism is not the same as other versions of utilitarianism, and, in the opinion of this author, it is superior to others. This Reader's Guide is intended to help readers of *Utilitarianism*, whether undergraduate students of philosophy, or professional philosophers, to understand Mill's distinctive theory and his defence of it.

CHAPTER 1

CONTEXT

'Ethics' or 'moral philosophy' – I use the terms interchangeably – is the branch of philosophy concerned with questions about what makes life worth living or not worth living, what are our obligations to ourselves and to other people, what is just and unjust in human actions and institutions. Traditionally it was an attempt to develop *theories* of right and wrong, good and bad in human actions and human life. Utilitarianism is one such theory, and John Stuart Mill's *Utilitarianism* is the most widely read statement of that theory. Actually there are many varieties of utilitarianism, and Mill's version is in some ways different from other versions. But his is one of the most reasonable, and his defence of his version in *Utilitarianism* is well argued.

In this section, I provide a context for understanding Mill's *Utilitarianism* by presenting it as one among many normative ethical theories and one among many varieties of utilitarianism. I then introduce Mill by giving a sketch of his life and writings and some of the elements of the philosophy of Jeremy Bentham, whose work Mill reflects and attempts to revise.

ALTERNATIVES TO UTILITARIANISM

Before putting Mill's theory in the context of alternative versions of utilitarianism, it is appropriate to put utilitarianism in the context of alternative theories of ethics. Utilitarianism is a consequentialist theory, claiming that actions – and laws, policies and social and economic institutions – are to be evaluated by their consequences; in Mill's version, by their contributions to the greatest happiness. '[A]ctions are right in proportion as they tend to promote happiness, wrong as they tend to produce the reverse of happiness' (Mill 1861a: 210 [II,2]; further references to this work omit the author and date). What alternative theory could deny this? Isn't each human being motivated to be happy, and to the extent that one is concerned about other people, shouldn't one be concerned to promote the happiness and prevent the unhappiness of others?

We can consider alternatives to utilitarianism in two ways. One is to think of the *structure* of the theory: not all moral theories take consequences to be fundamental. Another is to think of the *authority* of the theory. Some theories have a religious authority, or appeal to intuition or to 'natural law'. Let us first consider alternative structures.

One alternative is to make *duty* the fundamental moral concept. Such theories are called *deontological*, derived from the Greek word for duty, in contrast to utilitarianism as a *teleological* theory, based on the Greek word *telos*, which means 'end' or 'goal'. Utilitarianism, in Mill's version, has the end or goal of promoting the greatest happiness. Duties are derived from their contribution to that goal. A deontological theory views the performance of duty as the basic moral concept, not derived from what it achieves. Some duties are positive: to help people in distress; some are negative: not to kill, steal, deceive, coerce, or cause unnecessary suffering. Some are reciprocal: to show gratitude for benefits received and to make reparations for harms done. Performance of these duties does promote happiness and reduce unhappiness, but, according to the deontologist, that is not what makes them obligatory. They are duties in themselves and ought to be done, whether or not they promote happiness or prevent unhappiness. According to the utilitarian, duties are derivative and any so-called duty can be criticized. For example, if it is claimed that one has a duty to be loyal to one's nation, right or wrong, a utilitarian argument could be made that such a 'duty' is not truly a duty. A recognized 'duty' such as patriotism should be subjected to consequentialist evaluation. If it is claimed that if one has received a harm, one should harm in return, a utilitarian would question that.

Another alternative family of ethical theories is called 'virtue ethics'. For these theories the basic concept is neither action that is a duty nor action that contributes to an end, but the motive of the action: whether it is a manifestation of a virtue or a vice. Both consequentialist and deontological theories have a place for virtues

4

and vices. Honesty is the best policy, say the consequentialists; so honesty should be inculcated in children, praised in people of all ages and its opposite, dishonesty, is to be condemned. But for the consequentialist, honesty is instrumental: it derives its value from its effects. For the virtue theorists, the virtues are fundamental. Telling the truth does not derive its moral value from its good consequences or from the fact that it is a duty *per se*. Its moral value comes from the character of the agent that is manifested. If the agent is telling the truth because he or she is an honest person and that is part of the motive of the act, then the act has moral worth. For the utilitarian, character is important in judging people, but there is an additional criterion in judging actions. A good motive is not enough. Actions must be such as tend to have good consequences.

Consequential, deontological and virtue ethics are three of the most prominent types of moral theories in Western philosophy, but they do not exhaust the possibilities. There have been attempts to use the concept of *rights* as the most fundamental concept. According to rights theorists, duties and virtues are derived from respect for rights, and it is asserted that rights 'trump' the maximization of happiness. One is not permitted to violate a person's life or liberty, or – in some theories – property, in order to achieve greater happiness. It is also claimed that rights are the basis for the most absolute duties – not to kill, kidnap, enslave, or steal. The utilitarian has a place for rights. Security is an overriding necessity for happiness and avoidance of unhappiness. Mill will say that other benefits are needed by one person, not needed by another, and many can be cheerfully foregone. But security no human can possibly do without; on it we depend for the value of other goods, beyond the passing moment. So utilitarians such as Mill place great emphasis upon the respect for rights as fundamental instrumental values. But what rights are to be respected, and their respective weights when they are in conflict, according to the utilitarian, are to be decided by the consequences of respecting the rights and giving them their due strength against one another.

Still another model of ethical theory is based on the concept of a social contract. The idea is that I agree not to harm you under condition that you agree not to harm me. I agree to help you in distress under condition that you agree to help me in distress. Philosophers who take this approach do not claim that moral agents have got together to enter such an agreement. Either the agreement is regarded as tacit, based on receiving the benefits of living in a society in which the terms of such an agreement are in force and an individual in fairness owes the community reciprocity for the benefit received; or, it is regarded as hypothetical: it is possible to state an argument such that if one were to be able to enter into a social compact, it would be rational to do so. Therefore there is reason to act in accord with the terms of such an agreement so long as sufficient others are doing likewise. The terms of such a social contract would require people to attempt to achieve certain goals, in line with utilitarianism; it would require people to perform certain duties, as deontologists require; it would advocate that people develop dispositions to behave in these ways from sincere motives, as with virtue ethics; and it would require respect for fundamental rights. Contract theorists believe that the concept of a social contract provides a rational ground for the other parts of a moral system. Utilitarians think that nothing is to be gained by the idea of a social contract. They think that they have a foundation for duties and virtues and rights in their theory of intrinsic value, which is to be maximized. If social contract theorists arrive at utilitarian conclusions, their theory is not needed. If they arrive at non-utilitarian conclusions, their theory is perverse.

The preceding paragraphs have given a typology of the fundamental concepts of various sorts of ethical theories – consequentialist, deontological, virtue ethics, rights theories and social contract theories. Another way of looking at alternatives to utilitarianism is to look not at the fundamental concepts but at the source of authority. Consequentialist theories have a concept of intrinsic value, something valuable in itself or as an end that gives value or disvalue to the means to that end. Other sources of authority are intuition, the will of God, or Nature.

The intuitionist claims that one doesn't have to calculate consequences of actions. One just knows intuitively what actions are right or wrong. It is wrong to kill, to steal, to commit adultery, to enslave, to lie, to cheat, to break promises; and one knows this without having to think about the fact that these kinds of actions tend to produce bad consequences. But how does one know that? One account is that humans have a moral sense, analogous to the senses of sight and hearing, such that one can sense immediately that it is wrong to kill or to steal, etc. Another account is that it is not a sensory capacity but an intellectual one. One can recognize, without further argument, that there is a moral *reason* against killing, against stealing, etc. If there is a moral sense or innate capacity for accurate moral reasoning, the utilitarian will ask, why is there so much controversy over the scope of each of these concepts? Isn't the death penalty killing? Isn't killing in self-defence killing? Isn't killing in war killing? Yet these kinds of killing are hotly contested. Some intuitionists are absolutists, claiming that all of these are morally wrong. Other intuitionists intuit that some kinds of killing are permissible or even required. The intuitionist may recognize that intuitions come into conflict. The intuited right of self-defence may come into conflict with the intuited wrongness of killing. In that case, how does one weigh the conflicting obligations? The intuitionist can only appeal to the immediately felt insight of the moral sense or moral reasoning. The utilitarian has a more scientific alternative: what are the consequences for happiness of allowing or forbidding killing in self-defence and in what circumstances? The answers may be difficult to determine, but the utilitarian does not simply appeal to immediate knowledge – the utilitarian appeals to causal relationships.

Another alternative is the religious one. What is right and wrong is what God wills. There are (at least) two versions of this theory. One is that God is omniscient and benevolent. So God knows what is good and bad, and right and wrong, and wills the good and the right. If we can know God's will, we can know what makes life good and bad, and we can know what is right and wrong. According to this theory, to say that God is benevolent is a statement with significance. It is not simply saying that God's will is God's will. God's will does not *make* it good or right. God could be malevolent and will evil. But God is loving and wills the best for us. This religious theory has significance both for knowledge and for motivation. Not only can we come to know what is good and bad, right and wrong, to the extent that we can know God's will; we will be motivated to promote what is good and right out of response to the love of God and out of hope for reward and fear of punishment.

This religious theory is compatible with utilitarianism. If God is benevolent, doesn't God will the happiness of creation? Doesn't God will that people seek to be happy and to make others happy and to help them in distress? On the other hand, God may know that something other than happiness is good, and that something other than the promotion of the greatest happiness is what makes

7

actions right and wrong. And so this religious theory is also compatible with non-utilitarian theories of value and of morality. However, the diversity of religions, and the problem of knowing God's will – if there is a God – lead to problems with this theory. Mill also claimed that if there is a God, an intelligent designer of the universe, there is so much unmerited suffering that God cannot be benevolent.

A different religious theory, called the 'divine command' theory, is that it is God's will that *constitutes* good and bad, right and wrong. Independent of God, according to this theory, there is no objective value and no objective foundation for morality. An implication of this theory is that to say 'God is benevolent' is a tautology, for it is simply to say that God's will is God's will. God is by definition good. It is a contradiction to say that God could be evil.

A possible support for this theory is that if God is all-powerful, then God's will triumphs over everything. But this looks like 'might makes right'. Those who hold this theory usually reject that interpretation. They say that without a divine law-giver, morality is merely a human construct that is relative to human desires and aversions; to have objectivity, it must be grounded in something superhuman. The utilitarian response to this is that there *is* an objective basis for value in human and other sentient life. This basis is the fact that pleasure is objectively good and pain is even more obviously objectively bad. People do not arbitrarily choose to desire pleasure and to be averse to pain – it is a natural fact that pleasure is desirable and pain is undesirable. On this objective basis it is possible to construct an objective morality. The construction is not infallible, and it is not easy. There can be reasonable controversies as to what actions promote happiness and produce unhappiness, but these are controversies about the consequences of actions. They are not simply differences in subjective taste nor cultural conventions that vary from society to society. Divine command theories will be discussed further in the commentary on chapter 1 of *Utilitarianism*.

Another alternative to utilitarianism is the claim that what is natural is right, and what is unnatural is wrong. In his work on 'Nature', Mill points out that in one sense everything is natural, in that everything obeys the laws of the natural sciences. Another sense of 'natural' is the way things would be apart from human intervention. Mill argues that this is no basis for morality. All human action consists in altering the spontaneous course of nature. No one can hold that the whole of nature is good, with its diseases, earthquakes, floods and tornadoes. When people try to pick out which part of nature is good and which part of nature should be modified, utilitarianism has an answer: promote the greatest happiness. Any other criterion is arbitrary and based on prejudices. Things are called unnatural, such as homosexuality, artificial birth control, or polygamy, because they are unconventional. It is not that they go against nature any more than vaccinations and dental hygiene, they go against prevailing attitudes.

VARIETIES OF UTILITARIANISM

If a theory appeals to consequences to justify and to criticize actions, laws and policies, as utilitarianism does, it must have criteria for what are to count as good and bad consequences, and here there are disagreements among utilitarians. The 'classical' utilitarians including Jeremy Bentham, Mill and Henry Sidgwick (1838–1900), were hedonists. Hedonism in philosophy is the doctrine that pleasure and pain are the only things that are good and bad as ends, all other valuable things deriving their value or disvalue from their relation to pleasure and pain. Hedonism in philosophy is not the same as 'hedonism' in popular usage. In popular usage, hedonism often means attention to immediate sensual gratification without regard to long-term consequences and without valuing the pleasures found in intellectual activities, in the self-respect that comes from achievements and the fulfilment of duties and in intimate and enduring relationships with others in love and friendship. The hedonism of the classical utilitarians paid attention to all these sources of pleasure, not just immediate sensual enjoyments.

In the twentieth and twenty-first centuries, non-hedonistic varieties of utilitarianism have been defended, claiming that *sources* of pleasure and freedom from pain, such as knowledge, beauty, achievement of purpose, strength of character and loving relationships are valuable as ends in themselves, not merely in their relationship to pleasure and pain. In the early twentieth century, a non-hedonistic theory was called 'ideal utilitarianism'. Now the term 'consequentialism' is used to cover both hedonistic and non-hedonistic varieties, and 'utilitarianism' is sometimes restricted to the hedonistic theory.

Classical utilitarianism can thus be divided into two parts. One is the consequentialist view that actions, laws and policies are justified or not justified on the basis of their consequences. The other part is the theory of intrinsic value, that only pleasure and pain are ultimately valuable as ends, all other things deriving their value from their relationship to pleasure and pain. One could be a consequentialist with a pluralistic theory of value, including such things as knowledge, beauty, achievement of purpose, strength of character, loving relationships and so on, in addition to pleasure and freedom from pain. Still another consequentialist theory does not list the kinds of intrinsic value but regards desire satisfaction, whatever it is that satisfies desires, as the end value. John Stuart Mill, in *Utilitarianism*, however, is defending hedonistic utilitarianism.

Another important distinction is between direct and indirect utilitarianism. In estimating the consequences of actions, is one to estimate the consequences of a particular act in its unique circumstances, or is one to assess it as an act of a kind that generally has good or bad consequences? It may be that the only way that one can estimate the consequences of a particular act is to view it as an act of a kind that in the past has usually had good or bad consequences. For example, if one is contemplating whether to speed on a highway on this occasion, the only way that one can estimate the consequences is on the basis of the probability that one will have an accident, that one will be arrested for speeding, that one will feel anxiety from fear that one will have an accident or be arrested, and how much these are outweighed by the time that one will save or the excitement of speeding. The only way that one can calculate these probabilities is on the basis of the past occurrence of highway accidents due to speeding, frequency of arrests for speeding at this speed, past anxiety when speeding and so on. So it is on the basis of past consequences of actions of this type that one can estimate the consequences in this particular case.

On the other hand, there may be peculiarities in a specific case that make it different from the usual case: one may be late for an important appointment; one may be rushing a sick person to hospital. In those cases the time saved is more important than in the average case. One variety of utilitarianism, labelled 'act-utilitarianism', says that one should apply the utilitarian doctrine directly to the particular case: which among the alternatives in this particular unique situation will have the best consequences? This is a form of 'direct' utilitarianism.

Against this it is argued that if everyone acted on act-utilitarian calculations, some utility would be lost. If I lie to produce better consequences in a particular situation, it has little effect on the general practice of truth-telling. But if everyone does it, it weakens the general trustworthiness of human assertion.

Suppose, then, that I am the only one using act-utilitarian reasoning in a society that obeys accepted rules without calculating consequences in the particular case. One person speeding while everyone else is driving close to the speed limit is not so dangerous; so it would seem that one individual, in those circumstances, could justify speeding. But it seems *unfair* that one driver can be a 'free-rider' upon the law-abiding behaviour of others.

This lends support to 'rule-utilitarianism', the view that actions should conform to useful rules – useful being determined by the consequences of the general acceptance and practice of the rules. This is a form of 'indirect' utilitarianism. The utilitarian criterion of right action is not applied directly to alternative particular actions. It is applied to rules, and acts are judged right or wrong if they are in conformity with or in violation of the useful rules. Mill, in *Utilitarianism*, seems ambiguous between the positions of act-utilitarianism and rule-utilitarianism. The reader should be alert to that ambiguity.

For act-utilitarians, a distinction can be made between *actual* consequences and *foreseeable* consequences. This distinction, unlike the preceding one, is more terminological than normative. After the fact, one can look back and see that the consequences of an action were not what could be foreseen. If an action had bad consequences, but the consequences could not be foreseen, are we to call it a 'wrong' action? One way to express this is to say, 'I made the wrong choice, but I couldn't have known better'. Do we also want to say that I performed a wrong action? Suppose a friend asks you to help her buy a car. Without your help she won't be able to afford it and will have to continue getting around by bicycle. She is a careful driver and a responsible person, and your motive is to help her. Having bought the car, she is hurt in an accident that is in no way her fault. You may say after the fact, 'I wish that I hadn't loaned her the money. Then she wouldn't have got hurt'. Some philosophers say that your action was wrong but justifiable. You did what you believed was right and with good reasons, but it turned out wrong. It was a *rational* action but not the right action. Other philosophers say that your action was the right thing to do but unfortunate. English usage supports both descriptions, but for purposes of philosophical analysis the latter is preferable. It is simpler to formulate act-utilitarianism in terms of foreseeable consequences, for we can't do better in choosing what to do rather than in terms of actual consequences, which can at best be known only in retrospect. And even after the action, the actual consequences of alternative actions cannot be known. In the example of loaning the money to buy a car, if you had not loaned her the money she might have had an even worse accident on her bicycle. If Mill is interpreted as an act-utilitarian, he uses the word 'tendency' of actions to express the foreseeable view: the tendency of an action is what can be foreseen of the consequences of an action based on past experience. If Mill is interpreted as a rule-utilitarian, or at least not a consistent act-utilitarian, the tendencies of types of actions are the basis for the formulation of useful rules, which in turn determine right actions.

There are other variations within the utilitarian tradition by which we can distinguish Mill from others. These will be attended to as we examine the text in detail.

MILL'S LIFE AND WRITINGS

As said above, John Stuart Mill was the foremost British philosopher of the nineteenth century. His reputation was established by his *System of Logic* (1843), which is not only about logic in the narrow sense but includes a philosophy of language, a philosophy of science and a general theory of knowledge. Mill's 'methods' of inductive investigation presented in the *Logic* continue to be the methods of some twentieth and twenty-first century scientific and medical research. Mill's *Principles of Political Economy* (1848) established him as the leading economic theorist of his day. *On Liberty* (1859), his defence of freedom of thought, expression, liberty of actions and lifestyle that do not harm the legitimate interests of others, is a classic text defending those freedoms. And his essay *Utilitarianism* is the most commonly studied statement of utilitarian ethical theory.

Mill was born in 1806, his parents' first child. He had an unusual upbringing. He never attended school with other children; he was 'home schooled', as we say today, but he was not even allowed to associate with other children. He was tutored by his father, who in John Stuart's early childhood was a freelance writer. He was given an accelerated education. He was learning Greek at the age of three from vocabulary cards with the English words on the back – so he already knew how to read English. At eight he began the study of Latin. By that time he had already read, in Greek, several classics of Greek history and six dialogues of Plato. At twelve he began the study of logic, working through Aristotle in Greek and scholastic logic in Latin. In the year that he reached the age of thirteen, his father took him 'through a complete course in political economy' (Mill 1873: 31 [II, 11]).

The education was rigorous. '[N]o holidays were allowed, lest the habit of work should be broken, and a taste of idleness acquired' (Mill 1873: 39 [I, 24]). And he was kept from any association with other boys to avoid contagion by vulgar modes of thought and feeling.

Mill's father, James Mill (1773–1836), was a disciple and close associate of Jeremy Bentham, the founder of utilitarianism as a programme in philosophy and political action. In 1813, when John Stuart was seven, the Mill family moved to a house in London near Bentham's, which they rented from him, and each summer they would be visitors at Bentham's summer estate. But it was not until he was fifteen that John Stuart read Bentham's philosophy itself. In the preceding year he had spent six months visiting Bentham's brother's family in southern France, where he had learned French, and when he returned his father gave him a French translation of Bentham entitled *Traité de Legislation*. It contains much of the material in Bentham's *Introduction to the Principles of Morals and Legislation* (1789). In his *Autobiography*, Mill reports, 'The reading of this book was an epoch in my life; one of the turning points in my mental history' (Mill 1873: 67 [III, 2]). He was impressed with the way in which Bentham deduced from phrases such as 'law of nature', 'the moral sense', and the like, dogmatism in disguise, imposing sentiments upon others under cover of expressions that convey no reason for the sentiment but set up the sentiment as its own reason. 'When I laid down the last volume of the *Traité*', Mill writes,

I had become a different being. The 'principle of utility,' understood as Bentham understood it, and applied in the manner in which he applied it through these three volumes, fell exactly into its place as the keystone which held together the detached and fragmentary component parts of my knowledge and beliefs. It gave unity to my conceptions of things. I now had opinions; a creed, a doctrine, a philosophy ... (Mill 1873: 69 [III,3])

At the end of this section, some of Bentham's ideas that are related to the interpretation of Mill's utilitarianism will be summarized.

Mill's father had gained a position in the East India Company, a private corporation that managed British interests in India. When John Stuart was seventeen, his father secured a position for his son to work there, and he stayed for 35 years, eventually attaining the second highest position in the London office. Throughout those 35 years, and following his early retirement, he was extremely active as a writer of books and essays and for a time an editor of a radical political and philosophical review. Mill is unusual among prominent philosophers of the last two centuries in that he never held an academic appointment other than an honorary one. Perhaps this helped him to write for a wider audience. *Utilitarianism* was first published in *Fraser's Magazine*, a non-academic intellectual periodical. It was addressed to the general reading public, not primarily to students or professors.

When Mill was twenty years of age, there occurred what he labels a 'crisis' in his mental history. Some biographers have misinterpreted this as a mental breakdown. It was not. Mill continued with his usual occupations, carrying on his work at the East India Company, participating in a debating society and writing articles for newspapers and journals. Rather than a breakdown, it was a state of depression. He suddenly felt himself incapable of feeling the sympathy with human beings that was supposed to be the chief source of happiness of a utilitarian reformer of the world's institutions and opinions. After six months, on reading a memoir which told of a boy's father's death, the distressed condition of the family and the boy's making the family feel that he would be all to them, Mill was moved to tears. From that time the thought that all feeling was dead in him was gone, and he gradually found that ordinary incidents in life could give him pleasure. Biographers have engaged in speculation about how the event reflects on Mill's relationship to his own father. Mill himself drew two lessons from it. One was that happiness, as the end of life, could only be attained by not making it the direct end: those are happiest who have their attention fixed on other objects rather than their own happiness. The second lesson was that his own education was too narrowly an education of the intellect. He needed to cultivate emotions and feelings as well. And so Mill began to read the poetry of Wordsworth and to extend his circle of friends to those who were more poetical and less analytic than his Benthamite friends. He found, however, that they were often as one-sided in their views as the Benthamites, and Mill wanted to be many-sided. It was in this spirit that he wrote essays on 'Bentham' and on 'Coleridge', emphasizing to his radical and liberal readers some of the negative aspects of Bentham's views and the positive value of Coleridge's.

Mill also became acquainted with the writings of French intellectuals, including socialist thinkers and Auguste Comte. He had admiration for Comte's 'religion of humanity', but believed that Comte went too far in devotion to that ideal. Mill wanted to leave greater room for individual liberty of lifestyle, free from morality or religion, even religion of humanity.

One of the most important influences on Mill's life and thought was Harriet Taylor. Mill met her when he was 25 and she was 23. At the time she was married and the mother of young children. Both Mill and Harriet were already feminists, concerned about the subjection of women. They developed an intellectual relationship, and 21 years later, two years after the death of her husband, they married. Throughout those 21 years they were frequent companions and collaborated in the development of ideas that went into Mill's writings. Mill attributes to her co-authorship of much that he wrote, especially *Principles of Political Economy* and *On Liberty*.

Mill's first major published work, and the book that established his reputation as one of the leading philosophers of the nineteenth century, was *A System of Logic*, which appeared in 1843. The book had a rapid success, adopted as a set text at both Oxford and Cambridge Universities, and going through eight editions in Mill's lifetime. The title is misleadingly narrow, for it is a treatise that includes a theory of knowledge, philosophy of language, philosophy of science and much more. Mill's philosophy is in the tradition of British empiricism, stemming from Francis Bacon and John

Locke in the seventeenth century and David Hume in the eighteenth, with its emphasis upon experience as the source of the materials and much of the form of all knowledge.

In 1848, Mill published *Principles of Political Economy*, his major work in economic theory. This also had an immediate success and went through seven editions in Mill's lifetime. Mill pays unusual attention to the effects upon the labouring classes of various systems of property ownership, credit, allocation of resources and so on. Later editions become more sympathetic to socialism and more critical of existing conditions. Mill has in mind British and French socialist theories: he never heard of Marx and had no sympathy with revolutionary socialism.

Much of Mill's thinking was preoccupied with social and political questions. With growing democracy, Mill was fearful of the 'tyranny of the majority', not only through government coercion but through the informal social control of opinion and attitudes. His essay *On Liberty* (1859) attempts to draw a line as to what is appropriate for social interference and what should be left to individual choice. He is against paternalistic interference with adult behaviour when it is not harmful to others. The thesis of *On Liberty* is that the only aim for which mankind are warranted in interfering with the liberty of action of any individual is to prevent harm to others. The individual is the best judge of his or her own welfare, and if there is no harm to others, the individual should be left free from coercion, even if their behaviour is judged by others to be harmful to that individual. Mill's wife, Harriet Taylor Mill, had died before the publication of *On Liberty*, but Mill, regarding her as co-author, did not change a single sentence from her last reading of the manuscript.

In 1861, Mill published *Considerations on Representative Government*, defending representation as a way of making sure that laws are made in the interest of the governed. He also thought that active participation in elections had beneficial effects upon citizens, cultivating public sympathies and stimulating their minds. But he was also concerned to protect society from the ignorance of an uneducated majority. He sought to devise schemes for that purpose. It was also in 1861 that Mill published *Utilitarianism*. Between 1850 and 1858 he had written two unpublished essays, one on the foundations of morals and one on justice. These were combined into one work in 1859 and rewritten in 1861. The essay was first published in three parts, in successive issues of *Fraser's Magazine* (October, November, December 1861). It was reprinted as a separate work in 1863.

Two of Mill's lengthier but less frequently read works were published in 1865: *Auguste Comte and Positivism* and *An Examination of Sir William Hamilton's Philosophy*. The former contains admiring comments on Comte's 'religion of humanity', but criticizes it for making all actions matters of duty. For Mill, once minimum moral requirements have been met, there should be freedom to pursue one's private interests. Mill also has a class of meritorious actions that go beyond the call of duty; these should be praised, but their omission should not be the subject of blame. The book on Hamilton's philosophy is a source for Mill's theory of knowledge and metaphysics, going beyond the *Logic* in attempting to give an empiricist account of our concepts of matter and of our own and other minds. He attempted to reduce our concept of matter to experiences, calling a material object a 'permanent possibility of sensation'. The work, however, is primarily a critical attack on Hamilton as a representative of the intuitionist school of philosophy.

In 1865 Mill was elected to Parliament. He restricted his efforts primarily to the most unpopular causes and to those that had least support from either of the major parties. Most notably, he advocated women's suffrage. He proposed an amendment to an electoral reform bill such that women would be qualified to vote on the same basis as men. The amendment did not pass, but Mill was proud of his effort. When he stood for re-election, he was defeated, which surprised him less than his election in the first place.

In 1869 Mill published *The Subjection of Women*, arguing for equality in the marriage relationship, first class citizenship and greater economic opportunities for women.

In his last years he wrote an essay on 'Theism', which was published the year after his death, along with essays written earlier on 'Nature' and 'The Utility of Religion' as *Three Essays on Religion*. Mill had no religious instruction as a child, growing up an atheist. In these essays he admits that there is a possibility that the universe has an intelligent designer, but, if so, the designer is not benevolent. Nature, when personified, is cruel. He also finished his *Autobiography*, a classic of that genre, published in 1874, the year after his death. When Mill died in 1873, he was widely regarded as the foremost intellect of his time. He had a record of acute comments on the controversies of his day in culture and politics, and he had made monumental contributions to philosophy in most of its branches – logic, epistemology and philosophy of science; metaphysics and philosophy of mind; moral, political and legal philosophy – and to economic theory.

BENTHAM'S UTILITARIAN PHILOSOPHY

As previously mentioned, at the age of fifteen Mill had read Bentham's philosophy, and Mill was tutored by his father, a disciple of Bentham's. It is useful background to Mill's *Utilitarianism* to review some elements of Bentham's utilitarian philosophy. There is little doubt that this is the doctrine of utilitarianism that Mill has in mind to defend, with modifications, in his essay. Bentham's work that Mill read was intended as an introduction to a penal code, to give the philosophical foundations for a reform of criminal law. Mill, in his essay, is concerned more with morality than with law, but he and Bentham hold that the principle of utility is the foundation for both.

Bentham was trained in law, but he was independently wealthy and never practised. As a philosopher of law, he was appalled at the chaotic condition of the British legal system, and he sought a foundation on which it could be reformed. He found it in the principle of utility, a concept touched on by various writers but not, before Bentham, used as the basis for a systematic reconstruction of legal and political institutions and as the criterion for morally right and wrong action.

Bentham states the doctrine of utility in words that are reflected in chapter 2 of Mill's *Utilitarianism*. The principle of utility, which Bentham also calls the 'greatest happiness principle', is a principle

> which approves or disapproves of every action whatsoever, according to the tendency which it appears to have to augment or diminish the happiness of the party whose interest is in question ... I say of every action whatsoever, and therefore not only of every action of a private individual, but of every measure of government. (Bentham 1970: 12 [I, 2])

Bentham thought of happiness and unhappiness as simply a sum of positive pleasures and negative pains: 'A thing is said to promote the interest, to be *for* the interest of an individual, when it tends to add to the sum total of his pleasures: or, what comes to the same thing, to diminish the sum total of his pains' (Bentham 1970: 12 [I,5]).

An action conformable to the principle of utility can be regarded as one that ought to be done, or at least not one that ought not to be done; it is a right action or at least not a wrong action. 'When thus interpreted', Bentham claims, 'the words ought, and right and wrong, and others of that stamp, have a meaning: when otherwise, they have none' (Bentham 1970:13 [I, 10]).

Bentham said that the principle was not susceptible of any direct proof, 'for that which is used to prove every thing else, cannot itself be proved. A chain of proofs must have their commencement somewhere. To give a proof is as impossible as it is needless' (Bentham 1970: 13 [I, 11]). In chapter 4 of *Utilitarianism*, Mill addresses himself to the question 'Of What Sort of Proof the Principle of Utility is Susceptible'. Although he agrees with Bentham that his 'proof' is not a deduction from some more basic premises, he does claim that there is an argument for the principle of utility that can convince the intellect.

Bentham recognized that some people do not accept the principle of utility. Some oppose it, without being aware of it, by the very principle itself, calling it a dangerous principle. But this is to say that acceptance of the principle may have bad consequences, and what are bad consequences other than pains or loss of pleasures? Others oppose utilitarianism putting forward their own prejudices, their own feelings, as the criterion of right and wrong. Mill sees these people as his chief opponent in moral philosophy – those who claim to have a moral sense that immediately intuits right and wrong but that, according to Mill, really only reflects the standards of their society.

Mill's 'proof', as we shall see, is based on psychology, reflecting the dramatic opening of Bentham's *Introduction to the Principles of Morals and Legislation*. There Bentham proclaims,

Nature has placed mankind under the governance of two sovereign masters, pain and pleasure. It is for them to point out what we ought to do as well as to determine what we shall do ... The principle of utility recognizes this subjection and assumes it for the foundation of that system, the object of which is to rear the fabric of felicity by the hands of reason and of law. (Bentham 1970: 11 [I, 1])

Here Bentham is proclaiming two theses, which have been labelled 'ethical hedonism' and 'psychological hedonism'. The word 'hedonism' is from the Greek word *hedone*, which means 'pleasure'. Ethical hedonism is the view that pleasure and pain are the criteria the production of which makes acts right or wrong. Psychological hedonism is the theory that pleasure and pain are the ultimate motivational forces determining actions. One way of interpreting chapter 4 of *Utilitarianism* is to see psychological hedonism as the foundation for a persuasive argument for ethical hedonism.

If pleasure and pain determine what we shall do, it seems unnecessary to point out what we ought to do. The relationship, however, is not so simple. It is possible for an agent to choose an immediate pleasure that results in a loss of greater pleasure in the future or that results in greater pain in the future. A prudent person will forego an immediate pleasure for greater pleasures later on or to avoid greater pain in the future. Likewise, a prudent person may undergo an immediate pain to avoid greater pains or to achieve greater pleasures in the future. Examples are commonplace. If I am a student, I study today, even if it is unpleasant, to do well in the exam tomorrow. If I have a medical problem, I undergo an unpleasant procedure to avoid greater pains at a later date.

These future effects of my current activities cannot be predicted with certainty; so Bentham developed a 'hedonic' or 'felicific' calculus to enable a person rationally to apply his doctrine. In Bentham's analysis, a pleasure or pain has a certain intensity at any point in time, and it has a duration through time. These two dimensions constitute the quantity of a particular pleasure or pain and thus constitute its intrinsic value. Bentham did not draw graphs, but if he had done so, his graph of an experience would have had two dimensions. The horizontal dimension would represent the duration of the experience, the vertical dimension would represent the intensity of pleasure and pain. If one drew a straight horizontal line from a zero vertical point, that would represent neutrality between pleasure and pain – indifference between liking or disliking the experience. One could then plot a line with its distance above the indifference line to represent the degree of intensity of pleasure or below the indifference line to represent the degree of intensity of pain at any moment. If one subtracted the area between the indifference line and the pain curve from the area between the indifference line and the pleasure curve, one would have a representation of the 'net' pleasure (or pain, if it were greater), of any experience. We shall see in chapter 2 of *Utilitarianism* that Mill adds a complication. He believes that pleasures and pains differ in 'quality' as well as quantity and that the quality of a pleasure or pain affects its intrinsic value. Mill's view would require a graph of three dimensions.

Actions have pleasurable and painful consequences beyond their immediate pleasurable or painful feeling. These future consequences cannot be known with certainty, but their probability can be estimated. An action or experience that has only a 50 per cent chance of producing a pleasure of a given quantity has only half the instrumental value of one that would be certain to produce a pleasure of that quantity. What would today be called the 'expected value' of the former would be only half as great as the expected value of the latter. An action or experience may also have some probability of producing pains. So the expected disvalue of pains must be subtracted from the expected value of pleasures to give a total net expected value. Furthermore, an action or experience may cause pleasures or pains to other people. To take these into account, the net expected value for each person affected by an act would need to be included to give the total value of an act. Bentham said that it is not expected that this process should be strictly pursued before every moral judgement or legislative or judicial procedure, but he regarded it as the ideal towards which an exact process should approach.

Bentham, in his analysis of pleasures and pains, does not restrict himself to the pleasures and pains of the senses. He gives an extended list of pleasures: of sense, of wealth, of skill, of a good name, of power, of piety, of benevolence and so on – a list of fourteen categories, and for most of these there are corresponding pains. What Bentham does assume, however, is that all these kinds of pleasures and pains are commensurable – they can each be ascribed some intensity and duration as quantitative measures and summed up to give a total amount of pleasure or pain. Mill's position is not so simple.

Because Bentham holds a theory of psychological hedonism –

that pleasure and pain are the motives of all behaviour – pleasure and pain are the 'sanctions' that modify behaviour. Bentham enumerates four: the physical, the political, the moral and the religious. The first of these is simply causal relations in nature by which people learn that certain things cause pleasure and pain. The political sanction consists of pleasures and pains meted out by judges and other state officials. The moral or 'popular' sanction consists of pleasures and pains that arise from dealing with unofficial persons in the community. The religious consist of pleasures and pains expected to be experienced in this life or a future one imposed by a superior invisible being. Mill also has a theory of sanctions, presented in chapter 3 of *Utilitarianism*. Mill's theory is different from Bentham's in that he considers all of Bentham's sanctions 'external'. Mill introduces what he calls the 'internal' sanction of morality.

Mill modifies Bentham's utilitarianism in various ways: he introduces a qualitative dimension in his analysis of pleasures and pains; he has a more extended analysis of the sanctions of morality; he articulates an argument for happiness as the only thing desirable as an end; he has an analysis of moral rights that goes beyond Bentham. Nevertheless, there are more similarities than differences between the philosophies of Bentham and Mill. They are both utilitarians, and they both hold their philosophy in opposition to intuitionists and those who base ethics on divine command or on Nature.

CHAPTER 2

OVERVIEW OF THEMES

John Stuart Mill's *Utilitarianism* is an essay on the 'foundations of morals'. His purpose is to argue for the utilitarian approach to this subject. How does one argue in favour of an ethical theory? Basically, there are three ways. One can present the theory and answer objections to it. One can, in a positive vein, present its strong points, and one can present objections to alternative theories. In chapters 2 and 5, Mill is concerned to answer objections to utilitarianism. In chapters 3 and 5, he presents what he considers the strong points of utilitarianism – that there are motives for conformity to its principles and that there is a psychological argument in favour of its 'principle'.

In *Utilitarianism* Mill pays little attention to alternative theories. It is only in chapter 1 that he presents his theory in opposition to 'intuitive' ethical theories, briefly criticizing them. In chapter 2 he states the utilitarian 'creed' and considers various objections, such as that utilitarianism is a doctrine worthy of swine, and he attempts to answer them. These answers clarify and refine the utilitarian theory, both its claim that happiness is the ultimate goal of ethics and its use of 'secondary principles' for right action to achieve that goal.

In chapter V, he deals with the claim that justice is independent of utility and can be in conflict with it. This discussion is primarily an analysis of the concept of justice to show that it is not a simple concept in opposition to utility but that it is complex, divisible into a 'sentiment' of justice and a 'rule of action'. Furthermore, the 'rule of action' is not simple. In practice there are conflicting principles of justice, which are in competition with each other. To decide between them in specific areas requires a more ultimate criterion, and Mill claims that this is the principle of utility. Thus, in practice, justice is dependent upon utility for its implementation and the rules of justice, analysed as fundamental rights, are the most binding elements of a utilitarian morality.

Chapter 3 makes the claim that utilitarianism has an advantage over other ethical systems in sources of motivation to be moral, for with the advance of civilization and the interdependence of people, there will be an increase in the recognition of the identity of interests between them. Chapter 4 gives a psychological argument for the hedonistic foundation of utilitarianism. (Hedonism is the theory that pleasure and freedom from pain are of intrinsic value.) Mill claims that all people desire happiness and that desires for all other things as ends, rather than as means, are desires for things that can be analysed as 'parts' of their happiness (and avoidance of unhappiness).

This book will attempt to explain the arguments in each of these chapters in detail. Critical questions will also be raised as to whether Mill's analyses are adequate, his assumptions legitimate and his inferences valid.

In chapter 1, Mill is very brief. He contrasts utilitarianism as an 'inductive' or empirical ethical theory, appealing to experience, with the '*a priori*' or intuitive theory, which claims that we have a moral sense or moral reasoning ability that can give us moral rules. Because this discussion is so brief, I will draw on some of Mill's other writings to frame the debate. Elsewhere Mill has more extended arguments against intuitionism, and he also argues against appeals to Nature and to the will of God as foundations for ethics.

In chapter 2, Mill goes through various objections to utilitarianism. The most important of these is that in making pleasures and pains the criteria of the intrinsic value of human life, it is degrading, a doctrine worthy only of swine. To answer this, Mill claims that it is the objectors who degrade human happiness, thinking that humans are incapable of any pleasures and pains except those that constitute the satisfaction of animal appetites. Mill here introduces a notion of the distinction between pleasures and pain based on the 'quality' of the experience in addition to its quantity. This is an important departure from Bentham's utilitarian theory and will be given significant discussion.

Another important set of objections is that there is no time before acting for calculating the consequences of alternative acts, and that agents will find a way to rationalize action in their own interest rather than what has the best consequences impartially considered. To meet these, Mill calls attention to the need for 'secondary principles' based on past experience of the consequences of kinds of actions that have been found in general to have good or bad consequences. These secondary principles are the rules of morality that have been handed down from past generations. They are subject to improvement, but they are not to be dispensed with. The role of these secondary principles makes Mill a 'rule-utilitarian' rather than an 'act-utilitarian'. The issue of Mill's rule-utilitarianism will be discussed in the context of Mill's 'theory of life' that includes more than morality. It includes prudence and aesthetics and worthiness, also based on consequential pleasure and pain, but not enforced by punishment and charges of blameworthiness.

Some other objections that are addressed in chapter 2 are: that happiness is unattainable; that people can do without happiness; that it is expecting too much that people always act from the inducement of promoting the general interests of society and that utilitarianism renders people cold and unsympathizing. Mill answers each of these in turn, in most cases by clarifying the theory. For example, in regard to the first of these, Mill says that by happiness is not meant a life of continuous rapture, but a life of many and varied pleasures and few and transitory pains, and having as a foundation of the whole not to expect from life more than it is capable of bestowing. To the second of these objections, Mill says that utilitarianism does not require that people always act from the motive of universal benevolence. Most of our actions will derive from other motives so long as the rule of duty does not condemn them. The present work will discuss each of these objections and Mill's answers in detail.

In chapter 3 Mill is discussing what motives there are to be moral and, in particular, what can motivate one to follow a utilitarian code of morality. Bentham had listed various 'sanctions' – rewards and punishments that are conducive to moral behaviour. Mill regards all of those listed by Bentham – law, public opinion and hope of divine favour or fear of divine punishment – as 'external' sanctions. Mill is more interested in the 'internal' sanction – the development of conscience, the feeling of pain at the thought of immoral behaviour and of pleasure at the thought of doing one's duty. He calls this the ultimate sanction of morality. He claims that with the advance of civilization, human beings will feel a unity with each other that will promote a utilitarian morality.

Chapter 4 is Mill's argument in favour of hedonism – that pleasure and freedom from pain are the ultimate ends of human action. Although he says that it is not 'proof' in the ordinary sense but an argument to 'convince the intellect', it is highly controversial. This book will discuss some of the criticisms that have been made of chapter 4, but will conclude that none of them undermine the argument when given a fair interpretation.

Chapter 5 is the longest chapter and the most complex. Mill is attempting to show that justice is subordinate to utility, not a demand independent and possibly in conflict with it. He first distinguishes between the 'sentiment' of justice and justice as a 'rule of action'. He recognizes that the sentiment arises from an instinct that is independent of utility, but he claims that it needs to be moralized by being brought into accord with the rule of action. To understand the rule of action, Mill gives an extended analysis of the concept of justice, finally identifying it with a theory of rights. Justice is respect for these rights and injustice is their violation. But what rights people ought to have is a matter of what would be the consequences if those rights were recognized and enforced. Rights thus rest on a utilitarian foundation.

Furthermore, in particular areas such as punishment, taxation and distribution of collective benefits, there are alternative claims made by appeal to justice. For example, is it just to punish a criminal as an example to deter other would-be criminals or should punishment be aimed only at reform and rehabilitation? Regarding taxation, is it just to tax those with higher incomes at a graduated higher rate because of their greater ability to pay without as much sacrifice? Mill says that these questions cannot be answered simply by appeal to justice, for alternative answers can all claim justice in their favour. So Mill thinks that there must be a more fundamental standard to decide between the conflicting claims of justice. This, he claims, is utility.

Mill analyses justice, as distinct from other demands of morality, as a system of rights held by assignable individuals. However, these rights that are the substance of justice are the most fundamental of utilities, having to do with security. Most other needs vary from person to person and from time to time, but being protected from harm by others is something everyone needs at all times, and it is necessary for the enjoyment of all other good things in life. Thus Mill believes that he has shown that justice is not independent of utility but is a most important subordinate component of utility. In summary, commentary on chapter 1 will identify the theories that Mill thought were alternatives to his and give his criticism of them. Commentary on chapter 2 will discuss the objections to utilitarianism that Mill takes up, concentrating on his theory of qualities of pleasure as an innovation and on the role of secondary rules in his theory. Commentary on chapter 3 will give Mill's account of motives to be moral, which he calls 'sanctions'. Commentary on chapter 4 will give Mill's effort to support his hedonistic theory of value by a psychological analysis of desire. Commentary on chapter 5 will deal with Mill's analysis of justice as a system of rights and of how that fits into a utilitarian ethical system.

CHAPTER 3

READING THE TEXT

OVERVIEW: SUBJECT MATTER OF THE CHAPTERS

Utilitarianism has five chapters. Mill wrote the first four chapters intending them to constitute an essay on the foundations of morals. The fifth chapter, on justice, was written independently. They were combined and rewritten for publication. Chapter 2, 'General Remarks', is an introduction discussing the present state of controversy concerning the foundation of morality, and he introduces the notion of a proof of the principle of utility, in the wide sense of the word, which will form the topic of chapter 4. In chapter 2, 'What Utilitarianism is', Mill gives a succinct formula for the utilitarian 'creed' and then answers objections that have been raised against it, most of which were based on mistaken interpretation of its meaning. Chapter 3, 'Of the Ultimate Sanction of the Principle of Utility', is a discussion of the sources of motivation for conformity to a morality based on general happiness. Chapter 4 is entitled 'Of what Sort of Proof the Principle of Morality is Susceptible'. Here the 'principle of utility' is the claim that happiness is the goal, and the only goal, of morality, all other values being either 'parts' of happiness or instrumental to the attainment of happiness or the avoidance of unhappiness. The final and longest chapter is 'On the Connexion between Justice and Utility'. This last chapter takes the form of an answer to another objection to utilitarianism, but in this case the difficulty could better be described as due to an inadequate and incomplete analysis of the idea and sentiment of justice, rather than as a mistaken interpretation of utility, as in chapter 2. Mill's project in the chapter is to show that when properly understood, justice is consistent with, subordinate to, and an important branch of utility, rather than opposed to it.

CHAPTER 1: GENERAL REMARKS

Overview

Chapter 2, 'General Remarks', introduces the book with a discussion of the current state of moral philosophy and identifies the major school of thought that Mill considers to be his antagonist. In doing so, he characterizes morality as a practical art, which differs from a science. He ends the chapter by anticipating remaining chapters that will attempt to contribute something towards the understanding and appreciation of the utilitarian theory and towards such proof as it is susceptible. In reading this chapter, it is important to have in mind that an ethical theory can be defended both by giving its strengths and by stating the weaknesses of its opponents. Mill is here briefly identifying his major opponent and pointing out its weaknesses. The present work will identify other opponents as well and state what Mill considers their weaknesses.

I, 1

Mill begins by claiming that one might have expected more progress towards a decision respecting the criterion of right and wrong. He asserts that philosophers are ranged under the same banners, since Socrates, more than two thousand years ago in Plato's dialogue *Protagoras*, asserted the theory of utilitarianism against the popular morality of the so-called sophist. Mill does not state the arguments, but they can be briefly summarized. Socrates asserts that pleasure and pain are intrinsically good and bad: 'I am rather disposed to say that things are good in so far as they are pleasant, if they have no consequences of another sort, and in so far as they are painful they are bad' (Plato 1937: 120). Socrates then attempts to answer obvious objections to that position. Against the counterargument that people are sometimes overcome by pleasure in eating and drinking, which implies that pleasure is sometimes bad, Socrates argues that the evil is not on account of the pleasure that is immediately given to them, but on account of the painful consequences of their indulgence; and goods that are painful are not good for any other reason except that they end in pleasure greater than the pain, or they get rid of or avert greater pain. Socrates says that if you call pleasure an evil in relation to some other end or standard, 'you will be able to show us that standard. But you have none to show'. And, 'if you have some standard other than pleasure and pain to which you refer when you call actual pain a good, you can show what that is. But you cannot' (ibid.). In other dialogues, Plato rejects the *hedonism* (i.e., the theory that pleasure and pain are the only criteria of good and bad as ends) that Socrates here espouses. Mill does not claim that Plato or Socrates was a consistent hedonist. He refers to this passage only to show that the controversy between the utilitarian morality based on hedonism and its alternatives goes back to ancient Greece.

I, 2

Mill comments that there is controversy about the principles of natural science and mathematics. He does not give examples, but one might be: what is a number? Do numerals refer to non-physical abstract entities, and, if so, how are they known by our physical brains? This is a controversy in the philosophy of mathematics. There are also controversies in the philosophy of science. Mill says that the natural sciences and mathematics can be carried on without agreement concerning theories in the philosophy of science and philosophy of mathematics. The particular truths precede the general theory. Mill contrasts this with a practical art, such as morals and legislation. 'All action is for the sake of some end, and rules of action, it seems natural to suppose, must take their whole character and colour from the end to which they are subservient' (Mill 1861a: 206 [I, 2]; references to this work will omit the author and date, giving simply page numbers in the *Collected Works of John Stuart Mill*, vol. 10, followed in brackets by chapter and paragraph number). Mill continues: 'A test of right and wrong must be the means, one would think, of ascertaining what is right and wrong, and not a consequence of having already ascertained it' (ibid.). Mill is contrasting a science, which is a collection of facts, explained by a theory, with a practical activity, which, he claims, is an effort to achieve some end. The theory of what is the end would then precede any facts about how to achieve that end.

Is Mill correct about this characterization of a practical art, and is morality more like an art or a science? Creative arts, such as composition of poetry or music, would seem to be capable of being practised without a theory of creative writing or of musical composition. A literary critic or a musical theorist may be able to analyse the elements of effective poetry or of musical composition and, according to Mill's characterization of a practical art, they do not necessarily precede the practice of the art but, according to Mill, there must be a theory of the end for which the art is practised. Why aren't the arts like science? There is a practice of art that is recognized as effective practice, just as there is a practice of scientific research that is recognized as effective research. If morality or legislation is a practical art, there are moral judgements and legislative decisions in practice, just as there is scientific research in practice. Why are the cases not similar in that a theory of morals or of legislation is to be analysed from the practice, rather than providing a set of criteria preceding the practice?

In *A System of Logic*, Mill develops his distinction between an art and a science. He says that every art

> has one first principle; ... that which enunciates the object aimed at, and affirms it to be a desirable object ... Propositions of science assert a matter of fact ... The propositions of [of an art] do not assert that anything is, but enjoin or recommend that something should be. They are a class by themselves. A proposition of which the predicate is expressed by the words *ought* or *should be*, is generically different from one which is expressed by *is* or *will be* (Mill 1843: 949 [bk VI, ch xii, § 6]).

The role of science, on the other hand, is to show that certain consequences follow from certain causes.

If Mill is right that art defines an end, and the rules for practising the art are based on a science of the means to achieve that end, there is the question whether morality *is* an art according to this definition. Aren't there moral truths: it is wrong to kill, to steal, to deceive, to coerce, except in special circumstances? Aren't these moral truths? According to Mill's analysis of moral language, these are disguised as statements of fact, but are more like imperatives: thou shalt not kill; thou shalt not steal, etc. They are precepts or rules, rather than statements of fact. But they are not arbitrary. Arguments can be given to defend these rules and precepts, and it is the task of moral philosophy to support them with a justified test of right and wrong. Mill's theory contrasts with what is today called 'moral realism', a theory that draws closer analogies between morality and science. Mill claims that moral judgements, such as 'Killing is morally wrong', are to be interpreted as imperatives, such as 'Thou shalt not kill'. But what about 'Happiness is desirable and the only thing desirable as an end'? When we read chapter 4, Mill appeals to psychology. There he seems to be more like a scientist than an artist. He seems to be applying an analysis of desire to determine what is desirable. Mill, then, could be interpreted as an anti-realist with regard to *moral* judgements, but a realist in regard to *value* judgements.

I, 3

Mill will claim that the test of right and wrong is to be found in the tendency of actions to produce happiness and unhappiness. He sees the chief alternative to this to be the theory that we have a natural faculty, a sense or instinct, informing us of right and wrong without, in most cases, requiring the action to have a relationship to consequences. To kill is just wrong. To steal is just wrong. If this is questioned, the answer is 'You just know that it is wrong'. Mill says that those who hold this theory have abandoned the idea that the faculty discerns what is right and wrong in the particular case in hand, as our other senses discern the sight or sound actually present. 'Our moral faculty, according to all of its interpreters who are entitled to the name of thinkers, supplies us only with the general principles of moral judgments; it is a branch of our reason, not of our sensitive faculty; and it must be looked to for the abstract doctrines of morality, not for perception of it in the concrete' (206 [I, 3]).

But perhaps these thinkers have abandoned 'particularism' (i.e., the theory that morality consists of judgements about particular cases rather than of general rules) too hastily. Moral judgements occur in particular situations. These situations have great complexity. If I do have a moral sense, why may it not tell me what is right or wrong in the unique situation I am in: am I right to lie to a dying person about the bad health or criminal activity of her child? I may have a feeling that it is right or wrong in these circumstances without being able to formulate a general rule. Am I right or wrong to assist the suicide of a terminally ill person? There are many complex features of the situation. If I have a moral sense that it is right or wrong, can't that sense be specific to the unique characteristics of the particular case and not always the application of a rule?

Mill has not refuted such a theory. He dismisses it without argument. Instead Mill addresses those who believe that we have an intuitive faculty of general laws. He contrasts this intuitive school of ethics with the 'inductive' school, the utilitarianism that moral laws depend upon observation and experience. According to the intuitive, the principles of ethics are *a priori*. '*A priori*' means 'prior to' experience, not in the sense that its principles are prior in time, but that its principles are known independently of experience. An example of *a priori* knowledge, according to a common analysis, is the truth of arithmetic; that $4 + 5 = 9$ is not based upon the experience of counting four objects, counting five different objects and then counting all of them to see if one gets nine. There is a joke that if you put four rabbits in a cage (including males and females) and put five rabbits (male and female) in a different cage, and find, after several weeks, that there are more than nine rabbits, you do not conclude that four plus five do not equal nine. $4 + 5 = 9$ is not based upon the experience of counting objects but upon the definitions of '4', '5', '9', '+' and '=' within a numerical system. In the same way, Mill says that according to the intuitionist, the principles of morals require nothing to command assent, except that the meaning of the terms be understood. To kill an innocent person is wrong, based on the meanings of 'kill', 'innocent', 'person' and 'wrong' within an ethical system.

This is only one form of intuitionism. Another would appeal not to the meanings of the terms but to our immediate emotional feeling, our 'gut reaction' that some kinds of actions are right and some kinds of actions are wrong, and claim that this is a reliable moral sense. This form, along with the other, is susceptible to the criticism that it does not explain the great differences in people's intuitions, and it is subject to Mill's objection on the ground that morality should be progressive, capable of change based on new experience.

Mill says that both the intuitive and the inductive, as he describes it, hold equally that morality must be deduced from principles, yet the intuitionists 'seldom attempt to make out a list of the *a priori* principles which are to serve as the premises' of the moral system; 'still more rarely do they make any effort to reduce those various principles to one first principle, or common ground of obligation ... Yet to support their pretensions, there ought either to be some one fundamental principle or law, at the root of all morality, or if there be several, there should be a determinate order of precedence among them' (206 [I, 3]); and these ought to be self-evident.

Mill here is imposing his own vision of a moral system upon his opponent. Why need there be a self-evident single principle or decision procedure for adjudicating conflict among conflicting principles? There may be genuine moral dilemmas. To use an example popularized by Jean-Paul Sartre, the French existentialist of the mid-twentieth century, one may have conflicting obligations. Should a man leave his aged mother to join the Resistance against Nazi occupation? Or should he stay home and care for her? Sartre thinks that there is no rational resolution to the dilemma. The man simply has to choose, without being able to give an adequate rationale for his choice. So the intuitionist could say that the conflict is genuine and incapable of rational resolution. One knows that either choice fulfils one obligation while failing to fulfil another, but there may be no determinate order of precedence among them. Utilitarianism may provide a way of thinking clearly about the problem, by asserting that one should think about the probable consequences of alternatives to each of the possible actions, but Mill has not refuted intuitionism by charging it with the lack of a single principle or determinate order of precedence among conflicting principles.

I, 4

Mill claims that the principle of utility has had a large share in forming the moral doctrines of even those who most scornfully reject its authority. He cites as an example the 'Categorical Imperative' of Immanuel Kant, 'So act, that the rule on which thou actest would admit of being adopted as a law by all rational beings'. Immanuel Kant (1724–1804), German philosopher, sought to base morality upon reason alone. He was concerned that if one acted on the basis of the influences of one's heredity or environment, one should get no moral credit – the credit should go to one's upbringing, not to the moral agent. He conceived of a rational human being as a law-giver to himself. As a law-giver to oneself, an individual agent cannot make an exception of himself to rules that he wills to impose on others. Therefore he must submit his own motivations and intentions, whatever they happen to be on the basis of heredity and environment, to the requirement of universalizability. Kant thought that this would be a purely rational standard. Can the agent will without contradiction that his motives and intentions meet that requirement? Kant thought that all duties could be established by such a procedure. For example, he claimed that an agent cannot will without contradiction that he should never help a fellow human being who is in distress, for that would require that the agent will himself not be helped when in distress. But doesn't it depend upon the individual? Couldn't I will universal self-reliance? Mill claims that Kant fails to show that there is any contradiction in the adoption by all rational beings of the most outrageously immoral rules of conduct – universal selfishness might be an example. 'All he shows is that the *consequences* of their universal adoption would be such as no one would choose to incur' (207 [I, 4]).

As indicated, Mill thinks that his primary opponent is the theorist of a moral sense. The intuitionists generally take the received rules of morality as given, and these may be similar to what a utilitarian would advocate. But when attributed to a moral sense, they are not subject to criticism:

> upon the truth or falseness of the doctrine of a moral sense, it depends whether morality is a fixed or a progressive body of doctrine. If it be true that man has a sense given to him to determine what is right or wrong, it follows that his moral judgments and feelings cannot be susceptible of any improvement ... According to the theory of utility, on the contrary, the question, what is our duty, is as open to discussion as any other questions ... and changes as great are anticipated in our opinions on that subject, as on any other, both from the progress of intelligence, from more authentic and enlarged experience, and from alterations in the condition of the human race, requiring altered rules of conduct. (Mill 1835: 73–74)

I, 5

Mill says that on the present occasion he will not engage in further discussion of other theories. But in other writings he does.

Two other theories of morality, which likewise discourage critical evaluation, are the appeal to Nature and the 'divine command' theory of morality. The divine command theory can take two forms. Mill has no objection to belief that a righteous God would command what is morally obligatory and that if one could know the will of such a God, such knowledge would be informative of moral goodness. The problem with this theory is that there is so much dispute as to what God commands or even whether there is a supreme being. If it is believed that God's will is conveyed in a sacred book, there are conflicting claims both as to what book reveals God's will and conflicting interpretations of an accepted book. And those who claim to know God's will hold their beliefs in a way that prevents rational criticism. The other form of the theory is that God's commands are *constitutive* of moral obligation and of virtue, that there is no standard independent of God's will, that whatever God wills is thereby morally correct. One criticism of this theory is that the statements 'God is good, God is just, God is righteous', would then be trivial, meaning only that God's will is God's will. Another criticism of this theory is that there is no ground for morality except the *power* of God. 'Might makes right'. Both forms of the supernatural basis for morality are such that they protect it from being criticized. Mill advocates a progressive morality, subject to improvement with new knowledge and the reduction of prejudices. When morality is thought to be the will of God, the prevailing morality is immune from empirical criticism. Another problem is that if God is conceived to be the Creator of the universe, it is difficult to reconcile belief in a moral creator with what Mill calls the 'atrocious cruelty and reckless injustice' of Nature (Mill 1874c: 423).

This leads to another alternative to utilitarianism that Mill discusses in other writings, the appeal to Nature. In one sense all that happens, both human actions and non-human events, is a part of nature, in obedience to natural laws. When it means anything other than that, 'Nature' means what is independent of human intentions. Mill argues that this is irrational and immoral: it is irrational 'because all human action whatever consists in altering, and all useful action in improving, the spontaneous course of nature'. It is immoral 'because the course of natural phenomena being replete with everything which when committed by human beings is most worthy of abhorrence, any one who endeavoured in his actions to imitate the natural course of things would be universally seen and acknowledged to be the wickedest of men' (Mill 1874: 402)

For example killing, 'the most criminal act recognized by human laws, Nature does once to every being that lives; and in a large proportion of cases, after protracted tortures ...' (Mill 1874: 385).

Mill also thinks that the appeal to what is natural has had terrible social consequences and is a hindrance to progress. One of his greatest concerns was the problem of overpopulation. In this area an appeal to what is 'natural' has devastating consequences and needs to be opposed. 'Poverty, like most social evils', Mill says, 'exists because men follow their brute instincts without due consideration ...' (Mill 1848: 367–8 [bk 2, ch 13, sec 1]) When he was seventeen, Mill was arrested for distributing pamphlets with instructions on birth control, and later in life he asserted that facts regarding birth control should be communicated to married couples by their medical advisers (Packe 1954: 56–9).

In *The Subjection of Women*, Mill discusses the claim that the subjection of women is 'natural'. Mill points out that masters of slaves have claimed that their authority was natural, that theorists of absolute monarchy have claimed that theirs was the only natural form of government, that conquering races have claimed that it was Nature's dictate that the conquered should obey the conquerors. In general, those who wield power claim it as a natural right: 'was there ever any domination which did not appear natural to those who possessed it?' (Mill 1869: 269 [ch 1, par 9]). Thus Mill sees the appeal to Nature, natural law and natural rights as a hindrance to moral and social progress.

In the last two paragraphs of chapter 1, Mill introduces topics that will be the subjects of later chapters. Chapter 4 will give Mill's discussion 'Of What Sort of Proof the Principle of Utility is Susceptible'. He says that this cannot be 'proof' in the ordinary meaning of the term. It will not be a deduction from first premises. But he says that 'considerations may be presented capable of determining the intellect either to give or withhold its assent to the doctrine; and this is equivalent to proof' (208 [I, 5]). Mill will claim that the evidence for what is desirable as an end is what is desired as an end. He will argue that happiness is desired as an end and all other things that are desired are desired as means or as 'parts' of happiness. It is thus a psychological argument for the greatest happiness as the goal of morality.

I, 6

Mill here explains the task of chapter 2, 'What Utilitarianism Is'. He hopes to clarify the doctrine and dispose of objections that arise from mistaken interpretations of its meaning.

Critical discussion points: in this and other writings, Mill has identified alternatives to his utilitarian theory. Has he refuted them by saying that morality is a practical art, different from a science? Has he ignored the possibility that a moral sense may make judgements about particular cases, not just give general laws? Is it an argument against a moral sense theory to claim that its supporters have not come up with one fundamental principle at the root of all morality? Is it evidence against the moral sense theory and in favour of utilitarianism to point out that the principle of utility supports many of the moral sense judgements? Does an ethical theory have to be progressive, so that other theories that are not progressive are therefore false? Are his arguments against an appeal to divine will or to Nature effective arguments? All of these questions are worthy of reflection, but even if Mill has not refuted alternative theories, his own theory may still be the best. In the remaining chapters, he answers objections to his theory and attempts to demonstrate its strengths.

Study questions

Does an ethical theory have to be progressive?
Does an ethical theory have to have one principle at the root of all morality?

CHAPTER 2: 'WHAT UTILITARIANISM IS'

Overview
In chapter 2, 'What Utilitarianism Is', Mill is attempting to answer objections to the theory by clarifying what it is. He thinks that these objections are due to a misunderstanding of the term or of the theory it designates. In 'clarifying' the theory, however, he also makes revisions to the theory that he inherited from Jeremy Bentham. One of the most important of these is the claim that there are 'qualitative' differences in pleasures and pains that may make one pleasure superior to another independent of 'quantity'.

An important issue in analysing Mill's version of utilitarianism is the question whether he is an 'act-utilitarian', applying the principle of utility to individual acts in particular circumstances, or a 'rule-utilitarian', using the principle of utility as the criterion for identifying a set of moral rules having the best consequences and then judging individual acts right or wrong according to conformity with or violation of these rules.

Chapter 2 is an answer to a series of objections to utilitarianism. It is difficult to separate all of these, for they overlap. The following is one possible list: 1) that a theory that life has no higher end than pleasure is a doctrine worthy only of swine; 2) that happiness cannot be the rational purpose of human life because it is unattainable; 3) that people can do without happiness and to do so is noble; 4) that it is expecting too much to require that people always act from the inducement of promoting the general interests of society; 5) that utilitarianism renders people cold and unsympathizing; 6) that the doctrine of utility is a godless doctrine; 7) that utility is a doctrine of expediency in contrast with principle; 8) that there is not time, previous to action, for calculating the effects of any line of conduct on the general happiness; 9) that the utilitarian will be apt to make his or her own particular case an exception to moral rules. Mill attempts to answer each of these objections in turn.

II, 1

The use of the term 'Utilitarianism' to describe the philosophy that Mill espouses, although Mill takes pride in having introduced the term, is unfortunate. It calls attention to the importance of *consequences* by which actions are to be evaluated, but it does not convey the importance of *happiness* as a goal of life. Mill also uses the expression 'Happiness doctrine' to refer to the theory, but 'utilitarianism' is the more common term.

A common use of the term 'utilitarian' is to denote mechanical efficiency toward an end, devoid of aesthetic style. In this first paragraph, Mill tries to set the record straight – that pleasures of beauty, ornament and amusement are not excluded from the calculation of pleasures of a philosophical utilitarian. Epicurus, to whom Mill refers, was an ancient Greek philosopher whose name has ironically come to be associated with the contrary of his philosophy. 'Epicurean', in modern usage, refers to a taste for fine wines, gourmet foods and a lifestyle with little concern for the future. Epicurus himself, although a philosophical hedonist, asserting that pleasure and freedom from pain are the ultimate values in life, had the opposite advice for the attainment of pleasure and freedom from pain. He advocated a simple lifestyle of moderate drinking and eating of common foods in order that one not develop expensive tastes that one could not afford. The cardinal virtue for

Epicurus was calculating the consequences of one's actions, so as to avoid pains from such indulgences as intoxication and indigestion.

II, 2

In this paragraph Mill states a formula for Utilitarianism:

> that actions are right in proportion as they tend to promote happiness, wrong as they tend to produce the reverse of happiness. By happiness is intended pleasure, and the absence of pain; by unhappiness, pain, and the privation of pleasure. (210 [II, 2])

There are a number of questions to be raised about this formula. First, is Mill referring to individual actions or to kinds of actions? If he is referring to individual actions, Mill would appear to be an 'act-utilitarian', applying the utilitarian criterion case by case in unique situations. As we shall see at the end of this chapter, however, Mill says that there 'is no case of moral obligation in which some secondary principle is not involved ...' (226 [II, 25]). That would seem to make him a 'rule-utilitarian', applying the utilitarian criterion to develop rules, or 'secondary principles', with actions to be judged morally obligatory by virtue of whether they are in accord with the useful rules.

Another question is what Mill means by 'tend', when he says that actions are right in proportion as they *tend* to produce happiness or unhappiness. One possible interpretation is that some consequences of an act or kind of act are productive of happiness and some consequences are productive of unhappiness, and that these are the tendencies of the act or kind of act. The act would be right or wrong in *proportion* to these tendencies. An additional interpretation, however, even if it does not exclude that just stated, is that one cannot know for certain the effects of an act or kind of act. One can only know, from past experience, the probable effects. In his work *A System of Logic* Mill says,

> we must remember that a degree of knowledge far short of the power of actual prediction is often of much practical value. There may be great power of influencing phenomena, with a very imperfect knowledge of the causes by which they are in any given instance determined. It is enough that we know that certain means have a *tendency* to produce a given effect, and others have a tendency to frustrate it. (Mill 1843: 869 [bk 6, ch5, sec 4])

And in another essay, 'Sedgwick's Discourse', he makes a distinction between the accidental and natural consequences of action. In reply to the objection that for a utilitarian it is necessary to foresee all the consequences of each individual action, Mill writes, 'some of the consequences of an action are accidental; others are its natural result, according to the known laws of the universe. The former, for the most part, cannot be foreseen; but the whole course of human life is founded on the fact that the latter can' (Mill 1835: 63). Thus I think that the tendency of an action, as Mill is here using it, excludes accidental consequences and includes reference to what can be known of the natural consequences of the action or type of action, which can only be a degree of probability but is enough for the guidance of action. We can call these the *foreseeable* consequences of the action or type of action.

Mill uses the terms 'promote' and 'produce' in the expressions 'tend to *promote* happiness' but 'tend to *produce* the reverse of happiness'. Does he imply that one can 'produce' unhappiness and only 'promote' happiness? It is true that we have greater knowledge of what produces unhappiness than we have of what produces happiness, because individuals are much more alike in what causes them pain than they are in what causes them pleasure. This is especially true of non-physical pleasures, where there are great differences in taste. So we could interpret Mill to be making a distinction here. But I believe that he is here varying his terminology only for stylistic reasons to avoid repetition of the same term.

A critical question to be raised here and elsewhere in Mill's essay is his reduction of happiness and unhappiness to pleasure and pain. 'Happiness', in English usage, is usually thought of as a long-term satisfaction with life, whereas 'pleasure' is thought of as momentary. More will be said about this in discussing Mill's distinction between 'higher' and 'lower' pleasures.

In this paragraph Mill also introduces a distinction between 'the moral standard set up by the theory' and 'the theory of life on which this theory of morality is grounded ...' For Mill, not every action or type of action is subject to moral appraisal as right or wrong. Some recent discussions of utilitarianism make it out to be a morally 'maximizing' theory: if an action maximizes utility, it is morally right; if it fails to maximize utility, it is morally wrong. Mill's theory is not morally maximizing. He clearly thinks that not every act that falls short of best foreseeable consequences is a matter for moral condemnation. In his book, *Auguste Comte and Positivism*, Mill argues for a distinction between what is required as a duty and what is good to do but goes beyond the call of duty: 'it is not good that persons should be bound, by other people's opinion, to do everything that they would deserve praise for doing. There is a standard of altruism to which all should be required to come up, and a degree beyond it which is not obligatory, but meritorious' (Mill 1865a: 337).

This is a theory of what is sometimes called 'supererogation'. Acts of saints and heroes go beyond what is expected of ordinary people. They are meritorious and praiseworthy, but those who do not live up to that standard are not blameworthy. Mill clearly believes that moral blame should be limited to failure to meet obligations that fall short of the utmost that could possibly be expected.

In *A System of Logic* and elsewhere, Mill says more about the 'art of life' to which he refers in this paragraph. In the *Logic* he says that it has 'three departments, Morality, Prudence or Policy, and Aesthetics; the Right, The Expedient, and the Beautiful or Noble, in human conduct and works' (Mill 1843: 949 [bk VI, ch xii, §6]). The general principle to which all rules of practice in all three of these areas ought to conform, and the test by which they should be tried, 'is that of conduciveness to the happiness of mankind, or rather, of all sentient beings' (Mill 1843: 951 [bk VI, ch xii, § 7]). Value judgements in all of these areas are to be governed by the theory of life, 'that pleasure, and freedom from pain, are the only things desirable as ends; and that all desirable things (which are as numerous in the utilitarian as in any other scheme) are desirable either for the pleasure inherent in themselves, or as means to the promotion of pleasure and the prevention of pain' (210 [II, 2]).

But, as will be seen in reading chapter 5, there is a distinction between what is morally obligatory and what is generally expedient, that is, has good consequences without being morally required. Morality is primarily governed by rules that call for punishment if they are not followed. Other areas of life are admirable but do not call for punishment when one does not meet the highest standard of excellence.

II, 3–9

It is in these paragraphs that Mill makes his most significant revision of Bentham's utilitarianism. Bentham analysed pleasures and pains as having only two dimensions: intensity and duration. In these paragraphs Mill reappraises that to claim that pleasures and pains can have higher and lower 'quality'. The additional distinction is introduced as a reply to the objection that utilitarianism is a 'doctrine worthy only of swine' (210 [II, 3]). Mill's reply is that it is the 'accusers, who represent human nature in a degrading light; since the accusation supposes human beings to be capable of no pleasures except those of which swine are capable' (210 [II, 4]). 'Human beings have faculties more elevated than the animal appetites', Mill claims, 'and when once made conscious of them, do not regard anything as happiness which does not include their gratification' (210–11 [II, 4]). He cites the pleasures 'of the intellect, of the feelings and imagination, and of the moral sentiments' as having 'a much higher value as pleasures than those of mere sensation' (211 [II, 4]). Mill says that utilitarians have in general highlighted the superiority of these pleasures by virtue of their greater permanency, safety, uncostliness, etc. – the sensual pleasures are fleeting by comparison and often followed by pains. And Mill agrees with this assessment, but he thinks that there are some *kinds* of pleasures that are more desirable and more valuable than others. 'It would be absurd that while, in estimating all other things, quality is considered as well as quantity, the estimation of pleasures should be supposed to depend on quantity alone' (ibid.). By 'quantity' Mill evidently has in mind Bentham's dimensions of duration and intensity. If Bentham's pleasures and pains were represented on a two-dimensional graph, Mill's quality would require a third dimension.

Mill's evidence for a qualitative dimension is to assert:

> Of two pleasures, if there be one to which all or almost all who have experience of both give a decided preference, irrespective of any feeling of moral obligation to prefer it, that is the more desirable pleasure. If one of the two is, by those who are competently acquainted with both, placed so far above the other that they prefer it, even though knowing it to be attended with a greater amount of discontent, and would not resign it for any quantity of the other pleasure which their nature is capable of,

we are justified in ascribing to the preferred enjoyment a superiority in quality, so far outweighing quantity as to render it, in comparison, of small account. (211 [II, 5])

Notice an ambiguity in this statement. Mill seems to be saying that on any occasion that one could enjoy an intellectual pleasure, such as reading a good philosophy book, or one could enjoy a sensual pleasure, such as eating when hungry or having sexual intercourse, those who have experienced both would prefer the intellectual pleasure. If that is what he is saying, it is absurd. So let us give Mill a more charitable interpretation. He could be saying that people who have competently experienced 'the pleasures of the intellect, of the feelings and imagination, and of the moral sentiments' – the distinctively human pleasures – would not resign *all* of them for any quantity of the merely sensual pleasures. This is the interpretation that is borne out in the next paragraph. There he says 'that those who are equally acquainted with, and equally capable of appreciating and enjoying, both, do give a most marked preference to the *manner of existence* which employs their higher faculties' (211 [II, 6]; emphasis added). He says that few humans would prefer to be a lower animal; no intelligent person would prefer to be a fool; and no person of conscience would prefer to be a selfish and base person, even if they should be promised the fullest pleasures of a beast, fool, or rascal. Thus, Mill is not comparing higher and lower pleasures one by one, but a life of animal or base pleasures with a life that includes, but is not restricted to, higher pleasures. When seen in that light, the argument is more plausible.

When seen as a comparison between two manners of existence in which one is asked whether one would resign one for any quantity of the other, the argument can be turned around. Would someone who has experienced both the higher and lower pleasures be content to be deprived of all animal pleasures for any amount of intellectual pleasures? Would one for any amount of intellectual pleasures give up the pleasures of eating when hungry, drinking when thirsty, resting when tired, exercising when feeling the need to, getting warm when cold, getting cool when hot, and the pleasures of sex? The pleasures of the senses – seeing, hearing, smelling, tasting, touching, moving – are in humans accompanied by higher pleasures, the pleasures of beauty, conversation and achievement. But even aside from their human dimension, humans are animals and enjoy the physical senses. Isn't Mill underestimating this fact in his concern to deny that utilitarianism is a doctrine only worthy of swine? The richest life in most cases consists of a variety of pleasures, including those of the physical senses.

Mill says that the preference for a higher grade of existence is most appropriately called due to 'a sense of dignity, which all human beings possess in one form or other ... which is so essential a part of the happiness of those in whom it is strong, that nothing which conflicts with it could be, otherwise than momentarily, an object of desire to them' (212 [II, 6]).

Some commentators have claimed that Mill is here introducing a value judgement independent of pleasure and pain – that Mill has deserted his pure hedonism. Mill, however, attempts to give a hedonistic account. Whoever supposes that the superior being is not happier than the inferior being is confusing two very different ideas, happiness and contentment. A being whose capacities of enjoyment are low has the greater chance of having them fully satisfied, but happiness is not merely satisfaction and lack of dissatisfaction. 'It is better to be a human being dissatisfied than a pig satisfied; better to be Socrates dissatisfied than a fool satisfied. And if the fool, or the pig, is of a different opinion, it is because they only know their own side of the question. The other party to the comparison knows both sides' (ibid.).

When Mill says it is 'better' to be a human being dissatisfied than a pig satisfied, he is not just saying that we value a human being more than a pig. He is saying that the human has a higher degree of happiness than the pig. Whether a human can really know what it is like to be a pig satisfied is questionable, or even what it is like for an intelligent being to know what it is like to be a fool satisfied. But Mill is correct that a human can know some swinish pleasures, even if it is not the same as knowing them as a pig knows them. And a human can prefer to be a human rather than a pig.

Mill appeals to a sense of dignity, and I think that this sense can be given a hedonistic interpretation, even if it goes beyond what Mill explicitly says. The human psyche is complex. We not only have enjoyments and sufferings. We take pleasure or feel pain in what we enjoy or suffer. At the same time that we are enjoying a swinish pleasure such as sunbathing, we also feel pleasure or pain at the thought that we are getting a tan or risking skin cancer; that we are relaxing on vacation or wasting time that might be used more productively. At the same time that we are struggling with attempting to understand the meaning of life, as Socrates did, or devoting ourselves during a vacation to building housing for the homeless, we are thinking of ourselves as doing something worthwhile. The self-image that goes with any pleasure or pain can be a source of a 'second-order' pleasure or pain. I think that this is the role of Mill's sense of dignity. If one has a self-image that gives pleasure when one is engaged in exercise of the higher faculties, then, in addition to the 'first-order' pleasure of exercising the mind, of aesthetic appreciation, of social feelings or moral sentiment, there is the 'second-order' pleasure of thinking of oneself as having those thoughts or feelings. And if one is degrading oneself through overindulgence in 'first-order' pleasures of eating, drinking, or sexual promiscuity, then there is 'second-order' pain at the thought that one is doing so. When first- and second-order pleasures and pains are combined in a total experience, the quality (and the quantity) of the pleasure of the total experience is different from consideration of the quality (and quantity) of the first-order pleasure alone.

In thinking critically about Mill's theory of 'qualitative hedonism', there are (at least) three issues. First, are there qualitative differences between pleasures as pleasures, or are there only quantitative differences? Second, if there are qualitative differences, are some superior to others on grounds of quality? Third, if some pleasures are qualitatively superior as pleasures, are they correlated with distinctively human capacities?

Mill's claim that pleasures differ in quality is based on introspective psychology. If one reflects upon one's experience, having developed 'habits of self-consciousness and self-observation' (214 [II, 10]), Mill thinks that one can recognize that pleasures differ in quality as well as quantity. For example, if you reflect upon what it is like to feel the pleasure of solving a crossword puzzle, it feels different *as a pleasure* from the pleasure of lying down to rest when tired. I believe that Mill is correct in this. Some commentators have claimed that the sensation of *pleasure* is the same, only being accompanied by different non-pleasure feelings. In that case, the difference in pleasures would be only intensity and duration, with more or less of the unique feeling of pleasure. I ask the reader to reflect on this. Isn't there a different feeling of *pleasure*?

Other commentators have argued that pleasures are not

sensations, but the *liking* of sensations. They claim that sensations differ in the way they feel, but the *pleasure* of the sensations is the same – not an additional sensation but a degree of liking the sensation. In that case, the intensity of the liking would be the degree of pleasure, and it would not differ with the *kind* of pleasure. Again, I appeal to the reader. It is clear that in all cases of pleasure I like the sensation – for example, of completing a puzzle or of resting when tired. But does the pleasure consist merely in liking the sensation, or do I like the sensation because it is pleasurable? I think there is a sensation of pleasure as well as the liking of the experiences.

Introspective psychology is an appeal to self-consciousness and self-observation. If there are differences between two people's accounts of their self-consciousness and self-observation, it is difficult to settle the controversy. But I think that it is the only way to analyse the claim of qualitative differences between pleasures.

The fact that there is such a wide variety of experiences that are called pleasures is an additional fact that makes introspection difficult. We speak of 'being pleased' that something has occurred, such as that a particular candidate has won an election, and it is not clear whether this is the same thing as a felt *pleasure* that the thing has occurred. Being pleased seems to be more a 'state of mind' than a sensation or set of sensations that occur within a specific interval of time. But perhaps the state of mind is a disposition to have pleasure sensations whenever one pays attention to the fact that the event has occurred.

The decision as to whether there are qualitative differences may be clearer in the case of pains. Physical pains are generally recognized as sensations. And there is a vocabulary for talking about the qualitative differences between physical pains. There is a difference between a 'stabbing' pain and an 'ache'. There may be a difference in quantity, with the stabbing pain more acute, but there is also a qualitative difference. An acute ache, such as an extreme headache, may hurt more than a minor 'sharp' pain, such as the sting from a nettle. And a headache feels different from a stomach-ache, not just in its location within the body but in the kind of pain it is, regardless of intensity and duration. There are also psychological pains, such as grief or disappointment. They don't feel the same, and the difference is not simply a matter of one's dislike of them. I believe that introspective analysis should lead to the conclusion that there are qualitative differences between kinds of pleasures and pains. The reader should introspect and make a judgement.

Assuming that there are qualitative differences between pleasures, are some superior to others on the basis of quality? I may prefer one kind of pleasure to another, e.g., playing music in an ensemble to playing solo, but is this due to the qualitative superiority or to a quantitative difference. I may get more *intense* enjoyment from playing with others. Another problem is that people differ in their tastes; so there is no consistency in preference among a group of different people. There is also change of preference over time within the life of one individual. Still another problem is that it is difficult to separate the intrinsic value of a pleasure from its instrumental value. Mill appeals to competent judges, whose preference is of two pleasures 'apart from its moral attributes and from its consequences ...' (213 [II, 8]). This is a difficult requirement. For example, if one enjoys exercising for health, the pleasure is partially dependent upon the belief that it is healthful. In addition to having opportunities of experience and habits of self-consciousness and self-observation, Mill's competent judges must be good at analysing the desirability of an activity or experience into its component values, separating the instrumental from the intrinsic, and feelings of moral obligation from feelings of non-moral gratification.

Assuming that some pleasures are preferred as qualitatively superior, are these correlated, as Mill claims, with the distinctively human and the 'mental' pleasures, in contrast to animal appetites and 'bodily' pleasures? Are these distinctions correlated? Are the distinctively human all 'mental' and vice versa? Are bodily pleasures all gratification of animal appetites and animal appetites all bodily? There are some pleasures that humans can enjoy but which animals cannot, especially those involving the use of human language. Animals cannot do crossword puzzles. But some animals are quite curious and seem to take pleasure in satisfying their curiosity. Many animals show social feelings towards other animals or their human masters, and emotions such as anger, anxiety, fear of punishment and delight in reward. So the correlation between brutish pleasure and bodily pleasures does not completely hold up. On the human side, the distinction between mental and bodily pleasures is difficult to maintain. Humans when eating, drinking and having sex, do not simply engage in appetite satiation; they involve their 'higher faculties' while gratifying their 'lower appetites'. Many pleasures, such as appreciation of music and visual art, involve giving pleasure to the physical senses as well as intellectual and emotional response. So the distinction is one between poles of a spectrum with a great deal of overlap, rather than mutually exclusive categories. For the purpose of rebutting the criticism that hedonism is a doctrine worthy only of swine, the distinction is useful. But it is subject to criticism as a set of categories as to what pleasures are superior and inferior. Aren't there qualitative differences and qualitative superiority and inferiority among bodily pleasures? And aren't the bodily pleasures and gratification of animal appetites ingredients of a rich life for a rational animal?

II, 7

Mill addresses the objection, 'that many who are capable of the higher pleasures, occasionally, under the influence of temptation, postpone them to the lower' (212, [II, 7]). Mill's reply is that men and women often, from infirmity of character, choose a nearer good though they know it to be less valuable. But he denies that people

> voluntarily choose the lower description of pleasures in preference to the higher. I believe that before they devote themselves exclusively to the one, they have become incapable of the other ... It may be questioned whether any one who has remained equally susceptible to both classes of pleasures, ever knowingly and calmly preferred the lower; though many, in all ages, have broken down in an ineffectual attempt to combine both. (212–13 [II, 7])

A first point to make here is that we have interpreted Mill not as holding that every competent judge, on every occasion of choice, prefers a higher pleasure. Rather, we have interpreted him as holding that a competent judge would not prefer a life of exclusively lower pleasures. But is even that true? In other writings Mill affirms that people have a variety of tastes. Just as some people prefer rock music to opera, even if acquainted with and capable of appreciating both, isn't it possible that some people may prefer a life of sensual indulgence to that of the intellect, the arts and social activism, fully capable of all. Mill was brought up by his father with such strictness that he could not conceive of a voluntary choice of such a 'low' existence, but there is plenty of evidence of people capable of Mill's higher pleasures voluntarily choosing the lower – not, perhaps to the total exclusion of intellectual, aesthetic and social pleasures, but as the predominant interest of their lives.

Mill's claim that there are qualitatively superior pleasures was significant in some other areas of his thought. Bentham had said that quantity of pleasure being equal, pushpin (presumably some childish game) is as good as poetry. Even on Bentham's own terms, one would have to consider the consequences of the two ways of using one's time. Pushpin might be just as enjoyable a recreation, but if it did not lead to any further pleasures and poetry did, then in the long run poetry would be preferable to pushpin. Mill, using his theory of qualitatively superior pleasures, has an additional argument for poetry. The pleasures of poetry, making greater use of one's distinctively human faculties, have a higher quality as well as leading to a greater quantity of pleasures in the long run.

In Mill's essay *On Liberty*, although Mill does not use the terminology, qualitatively superior pleasures play an important role. The main argument of that essay is that individuals, if they are mature, civilized and of sound mind, should be left to make their own choices as to their life plans so long as they are not causing harm to others. The essay has complex arguments that cannot be addressed here, but one of the assumptions is that when people are compelled to conformity with custom or to the likes and dislikes of others, they are not exercising their higher faculties. Only when they are permitted to exercise free choice, to be original and creative, to make decisions about the truth of theoretical and practical matters, to engage in voluntary associations with other individuals and so on, can they obtain the greatest happiness. The greatest happiness, according to Mill, is not the satisfaction of *existing* desires, if these are uninformed. The greatest happiness is satisfaction of desires for pleasures measured by both quality and quantity, the qualitatively higher ones coming from the full development of individual capacities. He therefore advocates compulsory education to force children to develop the capacity for the higher pleasures, and he opposes the 'tyranny of the majority' when it attempts to force its lifestyle on people who want to experiment with alternative ways of living. Those who live uncustomary lives may be obtaining higher pleasures that the majority are incompetent to judge.

II, 8

Mill has a final note on the importance of competent judges who have experienced alternative pleasures and pains with habits of self-observation and analysis. Competent judges are required for quantitative distinctions as well as for qualitative:

> What means are there of determining which is the acutest of two pains, or intensest of two pleasurable sensations, except the general suffrage of those who are familiar with both? . . . What is there to decide whether a particular pleasure is worth purchasing at the cost of a particular pain, except the feelings and judgment of the experienced? (213, [II, 8])

II, 9

Mill says that if it be doubted whether a noble character is always happier for its nobleness, there can be no doubt that it makes others happier. So even without the notion of qualitatively superior forms of pleasure, a utilitarian concerned with the greatest amount of happiness altogether would advocate nobleness of character. This is an important point, not just for Mill's version of hedonism but for utilitarianism in general. Being a person of intelligence and conscience, even if the pleasures of this are not intrinsically superior, makes one capable of making greater contributions to the happiness of others. And this consideration shows that even if some animal pleasures are superior to distinctively human ones, a life devoid of the human ones is probably detrimental to the lives of others. If a person lived a life of total idleness, eating and sleeping, such a person would be dependent on others for his or her existence without making any contribution to their welfare. If a heroin addict could be supplied with a constant high, even if that state of existence held greater pleasure for him than any other, such a person would be parasitic upon the work of others and be making no contribution, or not a worthy contribution, to the happiness of others. One argument that has been made against hedonistic utilitarianism is that if there were a pleasure machine that, through brain stimulation, could give one greater pleasure than ordinary life, such a utilitarian would advocate going on the machine. The argument is that this is contrary to our intuitions of the good life. The 'thought experiment' of such a pleasure machine has a number of variations. According to one scenario, one goes on the pleasure machine for life, becoming almost like a brain in a vat with only a virtual life. In such a scenario, one is putting total confidence in technology to provide the good life and becoming totally dependent upon others. Such a scenario is subject to the objection that we do not trust technology that much, and we should not wish to be so dependent upon the work of others to provide for us. A utilitarian thus has arguments to say that the theory does not condone going on such a pleasure machine. But another scenario might be that one could get a dose of pleasure from an occasional stint on the machine without becoming totally addicted to it and such that one could live a normal life the rest of the time, using the machine only for recreation. In that case, it isn't so counter-intuitive as a bad thing. It might be much more healthful than the use of alcohol.

II, 10

Having introduced qualitative distinctions among pleasures and pains, Mill restates the Greatest Happiness Principle:

> the ultimate end, with reference to and for the sake of which all other things are desirable (whether we are considering our own good or that of other people), is an existence exempt as far as possible from pain, and as rich as possible in enjoyments, both in point of quantity and quality; the test of quality, and the rule for measuring it against quantity, being the preference felt by those who, in their opportunities of experience, to which must be added their habits of self-consciousness and self-observation, are best furnished with the means of comparison. (214, [II, 10])

This being the end of human action

> is necessarily also the standard of morality; which may accordingly be defined, the rules and precepts for human conduct, by the observance of which an existence such as has been described might be, to the greatest extent possible, secured to all mankind; and not to them only, but so far as the nature of things admits, to the whole sentient creation. (214 [II, 10])

Notice that Mill is not anthropocentric – that is, he does not limit his morality to concern for human beings. All sentient beings, to the extent that they can experience pleasure and pain, are to be included in utilitarian calculations. Is this correct? Do non-human animals, to the extent that they can experience pleasure and pain, count? Most utilitarians who address issues in environmental ethics say that non-human sentience counts. It is difficult to measure pleasures and pains of rats and mice against the pleasures and pains of humans who find them a nuisance or destructive of human assets, or for whom medical research using them has promise of discoveries helpful to humans, but their pleasures and pains do count. Some utilitarians have been among the most vocal in objecting to methods of factory farming and to medical research that causes animal suffering.

On the other hand, there is no indication that Mill, although he did not address the issue, would regard non-sentient entities, such as plants and species and eco-systems, as having intrinsic worth. He would regard extinction of a species as a loss to human contemplation. Mill was an amateur botanist and appreciated the vast variety of plant life. To the extent that the extinction of a form of plant or animal life or of an ecosystem affected the pleasures and pains of human and non-human sentient beings, that should be taken into account, but there is no indication that he regarded the continuation of a species as in itself valuable. If this is the correct interpretation of the implications of Mill's position, is it correct? Is the extinction of a species a loss of something of intrinsic not just instrumental value? What about cultural artefacts? Many languages are becoming extinct. If no one cares, including those who spoke the language, is this a loss? It removes some of the complexity of human culture that could be of interest to anthropologists and linguists, but is it a loss in itself?

II, 11–14

A second major objection to utilitarianism that Mill considers is the claim that happiness cannot be the rational purpose of human life and action because it is unattainable, that men can do without happiness, and that renunciation of happiness is the necessary condition of all virtue.

II, 12

Mill points out that utility includes not only the pursuit of happiness but the prevention and mitigation of unhappiness; so as long as mankind think fit to live at all, not taking refuge in suicide, as recommended under certain conditions by Novalis (1772–1801), a German Romantic poet-philosopher.

When it is said that happiness is impossible, Mill thinks that this is a misunderstanding of happiness. 'If by happiness be meant a continuity of highly pleasurable excitement, it is evident that this is impossible' (215 [II, 12]). But those who think that happiness is the end of life mean by happiness 'not a life of rapture; but moments of such, in an existence made up of few and transitory pains, many and various pleasures, with a decided predominance of the active over the passive, and having as the foundation of the whole, not to expect more from life than it is capable of bestowing' (ibid.).

Mill claims that such a life is now the lot of many during a considerable portion of their lives. 'The present wretched education, and wretched social arrangements, are the only real hindrance to its being attainable by almost all' (ibid.).

Mill was a social reformer. He participated in the efforts of the 'philosophical radicals', a reform movement, to abolish tariffs on the importation of grain, in the belief that cheaper food would benefit the working classes, and to extend the right to vote to the working classes, in the belief that with the vote they could get legislation that would better reflect their interests. In his *Principles of Political Economy*, first published in 1848 and going through seven editions in Mill's lifetime, he pays unusual attention to the effects upon the labouring classes of various systems of property ownership, credit, allocation of resources and changes in industrial and agricultural productivity. Mill attempted to make a distinction between the laws of the production of wealth, dependent on the properties of objects, and the modes of distribution, which to a greater extent depend upon human will. Modes of distribution do not depend on necessities of nature but on those combined with the existing arrangements of society, and can be altered by the progress of social improvement. In the year in which I write this book, the richest two per cent of the world's population owns one half of the world's wealth, while the poorest half of the world's population owns only one per cent. This distribution of wealth is appalling to a utilitarian concerned with the greatest happiness, for the poor are those who could most improve their happiness by having more wealth, and the richest are those whose happiness would be least affected by having less wealth.

This is a symptom of the wretched social conditions that Mill is referring to in saying that wretched social conditions are preventing more people from enjoying happiness. Later editions of the *Principles of Political Economy* were more sympathetic to socialism and more critical of existing conditions. He had in mind the 'utopian' socialists of the middle of the nineteenth century, not revolutionary Marxists; Mill did not know of Marx, and he dismissed revolutionary socialists as advocating terrible violence with the unrealistic hope that it would introduce some new order. Even regarding the socialists to whom Mill was sympathetic, he was fearful that they restrained liberty too much, requiring collective uniformity. Still, he believed that their ideas should be tested in practice. He says that the social problem of the future would be how to unite the greatest individual liberty of action with a common ownership in the raw materials of the globe, and an equal participation of all in the benefits of combined labour. Notice his radical vision of public ownership in the raw materials of the globe – the fields, forests, mines, waters, and so on. He thought that any appropriation of privately owned property should be compensated, but he also believed that inheritance rights should be limited. No one should be able to inherit or receive by gift more than enough personally to live a comfortable lifestyle. The amassing of fortunes, passed on to one's descendents, worked against the general happiness. What do you think of these proposals as applications of utilitarianism? Would they make for the greatest happiness?

Another of the wretched social arrangements that occupied Mill was the oppression of women. He wrote a book, *The Subjection of Women*, in which he argued in favour of equality in the marriage relationship, first-class citizenship and greater economic opportunities for women. When he served in Parliament, he introduced a bill to extend the vote to women on the same basis as for men. He believed that half the population was deprived of its share of happiness due to unfair treatment. Is Mill correct in this concern for the subjection of women? Is it possible for women, so long as they must bear children, to be equal in the family and in employment? Should women consider it their natural role to be mothers and care-providers? Is there unfair treatment of women in marriage and in employment?

Two of the greatest obstacles to a more extensive share of happiness, according to Mill, are the lack of universal education and the lack of the practice of family planning. Mill advocated compulsory education for children, with public subsidy to pay for the education of those unable to pay for it themselves. Universal literacy would open opportunities not only for better employment but make life more enjoyable with greater access to the higher pleasures. Family planning would enable families better to provide for their children and reduce unemployment. If there was a shortage of labour, workers could bargain up their wages in order to have a higher standard of living. Family planning would also give women, who carry the chief burden of parenting, greater freedom. Is Mill correct about this?

II, 13

Mill says that the main constituents of a satisfied life are a combination of tranquillity and excitement. 'With much tranquillity, many find that they can be content with very little pleasure: with much excitement, many can reconcile themselves to a considerable quantity of pain' (215 [II, 13]).

He also analyses the chief cause of unhappiness, for those who are tolerably fortunate in their outward lot, in selfishness. One great source of happiness is sympathy with the happiness of others, and one can endure periods of depression or pain if one can find pleasure in such sympathy. Next to selfishness, he says that the principal cause is lack of mental cultivation. 'A cultivated mind', he says, 'finds sources of inexhaustible interest in all that surrounds it; in the objects of nature, the achievements of art, the imaginations of poetry, the incidents of history, the ways of mankind past and present, and their prospects in the future' (216 [II, 13]).

II, 14

Mill sees no reason why an amount of mental culture sufficient to give an intelligent person interest in these objects should not be the inheritance of everyone born in a civilized country, nor does he see any necessity why anyone should be a selfish egotist, 'unless such a person, through bad laws, or subjection to the will of others, is denied the liberty to use the sources of happiness within his reach . . .' (216 [II, 14]). The main problem is to eliminate the great sources of physical and mental suffering, such as poverty, disease and the premature loss of objects of one's affection. Mill believes that these can be reduced or eliminated.

II, 15–17

Mill next turns to the part of the objection that says that people have an obligation to do without happiness. He recognizes that it is possible to do without happiness. Many people do so involuntarily, and the hero or the martyr does so voluntarily for something that he or she prizes more than happiness. Mill says that the utilitarian acknowledges that the readiness to serve the happiness of others by the absolute sacrifice of one's own is the highest virtue that can be found in man. But utilitarianism refuses to admit that sacrifice is itself a good. 'A sacrifice which does not increase, or tend to increase, the sum total of happiness, it considers as wasted. The only self-renunciation which it applauds, is devotion to the happiness, or some of the means of happiness, of others; either of mankind collectively, or of individuals within the limits imposed by the collective interests of mankind' (218 [11, 17]).

II, 18

Mill reminds the reader that the happiness which is the utilitarian standard of right conduct is not the agent's own happiness, but that of all concerned. 'As between his own happiness and that of others, utilitarianism requires him to be as strictly impartial as a disinterested and benevolent spectator. In the golden rule of Jesus of Nazareth, we read the complete spirit of the ethics of utility. To do as one would be done by, and to love one's neighbour as oneself, constitute the ideal perfection of utilitarian morality' (218 [II, 18]). The utilitarian will also support laws and social arrangements to harmonize the interests of every individual with that of all and seek through education and opinion to establish an association between the happiness of each and the good of others.

II, 19

Another object, which follows from the point just made, is that it is expecting too much to require that people always act from the motive of promoting the general happiness. To answer this, Mill makes two points. The first is a distinction between the standard of right and wrong action on the one hand and, on the other hand, the various motives that may induce people to act as they do. 'It is the business of ethics', Mill says, 'to tell us what are our duties, or by what test we may know them; but no system of ethics requires that the sole motive of all we do shall be a feeling of duty; on the contrary, ninety-nine hundredths of all our actions are done from other motives, and rightly so done, if the rule of duty does not condemn them' (219 [II, 19]).

For example, many of one's daily tasks are done from motives such as to perform one's job well, or to eat healthy food, without having to think about whether it is one's duty to do so. The basic motive may be self-regard. If I don't do my job well, I may lose it. If I don't eat healthy foods, I may get sick. I don't have to think about whether these are maximizing the general happiness so long as they are not in conflict with my obligations to others. The second point that Mill makes is that even when acting 'from the motive of duty, and in direct obedience to principle', it is usually not necessary 'that people should fix their minds upon so wide a generality as the world or society at large. The great majority of good acts are intended, not for the benefit of the world, but for that of individuals, of which the good of the world is made up ...' (220 [II, 19]).

Mill says that 'the occasions on which any person (except one in a thousand) has it in his power to do [good] on an extended scale, in other words, to be a public benefactor, are but exceptional; and on these occasions alone is he called on to consider public utility; in every other case, private utility, the interest or happiness of some few persons, is all he has to attend to' (220 [II, 19]).

Thus, the utilitarian does not call on people to sacrifice the welfare of their families in order to help those who are in need somewhere else on the globe. Charity is an obligation for a utilitarian, but not at the expense of those close by who need and can benefit from one's close attention. One can generally do more good by helping those who are dependent upon oneself, or whose needs one is knowledgeable about, such as family, friends and close acquaintances, than by giving of one's resources beyond a certain point to general human or animal needs. This, however, is a controversial point. It may be that we use the argument that those who are close by need our care as an immoral excuse not to do enough for the dire needs of strangers. Aren't there responsible organizations with the information necessary to be effective in meeting the needs of some of the poorest people on earth? Wouldn't it contribute more to the general happiness if I gave more to these organizations than for me to give to local charities? And wouldn't it do more for the general happiness, impartially considered, if I gave more to charity and spent less on my own comfortable lifestyle?

Mill says that 'utilitarian moralists have gone beyond almost all others in affirming that the motive has nothing to do with the morality of the action, though much with the worth of the agent. He who saves a fellow creature from drowning does what is morally right, whether his motive be duty, or the hope of being paid for his trouble ...' (219 [II, 19]). In this respect, the utilitarian moralists that Mill identifies with hold a position contrary to popular morality, in Mill's time and today. Generally it is thought that the motive of an action is part of what makes it right or wrong. This is one of the differences between 'virtue ethics' and utilitarianism. Virtue ethics defines actions as right or wrong according to whether they express proper or improper motives. Mill attempts to define an action as right or wrong according to its consequences, making the motive of the action relevant only to the appraisal of the agent. Utilitarians do regard some motives as good and some motives as bad. Those motives that tend to have good consequences are good, and those that tend to have bad consequences are bad. And agents with good motives are to be admired and praised, and those with bad motives are to be despised and blamed.

Part of the problem of whether the motive is relevant is the question of how to describe an action. If I have a colleague who is ill and I telephone her from the motive of genuine concern about her condition and a desire to cheer her up, is that the same act as if I telephone her because, when she returns to work, she will ask why I didn't ever call? In the first case, it is an act of kindness; in the second, it is an act of self-regard. They both are acts of telephoning to enquire about the condition of a sick colleague, but is that a complete description of the act? In a footnote to a revised edition of Mill's essay, he discusses the difference between the cases of saving someone from drowning from duty, and a tyrant who saves someone from drowning in order to torture him. Mill answers by a distinction between the *intention* of the agent and the agent's *motive*. The intention is what the agent *wills to do*; the motive is the feeling that makes him will to do it. In the case of telephoning my colleague who is ill, Mill might try to differentiate the acts by their intentions: in the one case my intention is to cheer up my colleague; in the other case my intention is to avoid embarrassment. Can what one wills to do be separated from the 'feeling' which motivates what one wills to do? Isn't kindness both a motive – a feeling – but also a will to do certain kinds of acts? Beneficence is a motive – the motive to *will the welfare of others*. The reader can reflect upon whether this distinction between motive and intention can be maintained. In some cases, however, it is useful to distinguish description of the motive from the description of the action. We can talk of good deeds being done from bad motives and bad deeds being done from good motives. An over-protective parent may bring up a child in a way that is damaging to the child's self-confidence. The motive (or intention) is a good one: concern for the safety and welfare of the child (with that intention). But if it is counter-productive, having the opposite consequences, we can say that it is the wrong way to rear the child. We can then praise the parent for the parent's motive, but criticize the parent's actions.

On the second point of this paragraph – that most of our actions are done from motives other than a feeling of duty – Mill says that in most cases private utility, the interest or happiness of some few persons, is all we have to attend to. But, he says, 'of things which people forbear to do, from moral considerations, though the consequences in the particular case might be beneficial – it would be unworthy of an intelligent agent not to be consciously aware that the action is of a class which, if practiced generally, would be generally injurious, and that this is the ground of the obligation to abstain from it' (220 [II 19]). This passage is one of those in which Mill clearly seems to be a rule-utilitarian. If an action is such that its *general practice* would have bad consequences, and for that reason there are moral considerations against it, one has a ground of obligation to abstain from it '*though the consequences in the particular case might be beneficial*' (ibid., emphasis added). Here, where there are moral considerations based on the general practice, Mill is clearly rejecting a thoroughly act-utilitarian application of utility to the particular case.

II, 20–21

Another objection is that utilitarianism renders people cold and unsympathizing, making them regard only the consequences of actions, not taking into account the qualities from which those actions emanate. Mill's reply to this is to distinguish again between the morality of an action and the character of the person who performs it. An action is not right or wrong because of the motive from which it is done, but because of its consequences. Mill reminds us that there is nothing in the utilitarian theory inconsistent with the fact that there are other things that interest us in persons besides the rightness or wrongness of their actions. The Stoics (a tradition in philosophy in ancient Greece and Rome) attempted to make the virtue of the agent the criterion of morality as well as the standard of value of the agent, but that is not true of most moral systems, including utilitarianism. 'Utilitarians are quite aware that there are other desirable possessions and qualities besides virtue, and are perfectly willing to allow to all of them their full worth' (221 [II, 20]). Mill says that some utilitarians may have concentrated too much on the morality of actions, to the exclusion of other beauties of character that go towards making a human being loveable or admirable but, as with adherents of other systems, 'there is every imaginable degree of rigidity and of laxity in the application of their standard' (221 [II, 21]).

II, 22

Another objection is that the doctrine of utility is a *godless* doctrine. To this Mill replies that the question depends upon what idea we have formed of the moral character of the Deity. 'If it be a true belief that God desires, above all things, the happiness of his creatures, and that this was his purpose in their creation, utility is not only not a godless doctrine, but more profoundly religious than any other' (222 [II, 22]). In this reply, Mill is really evading the charge. It may be possible to say that there is nothing in utilitarianism that makes it incompatible with the belief in God, but unlike religious foundations for morality, utilitarianism does not depend upon any belief in a deity for the standard of morality or for the sanctions of morality. As indicated in discussing Mill's life and the alternatives to utilitarianism, Mill had no belief in a supernatural being, and he thought that religious morality, including Christian morality, was misguided. Mill admired the teaching of Jesus that one should love one's neighbour as oneself. But he believed that the teaching had been corrupted by Christian traditions and belief in a divine Providence controlling history and people's lives. The tradition of divine retribution, condemning people to eternal punishment for their sins, and the belief that there is a natural law prohibiting various unconventional modes of conduct, such as artificial birth control, were among the targets of Mill's philosophy. The only God that Mill could respect would be one that was benevolent, and Mill could not find evidence for benevolence in the course of nature. Any intelligent designer of the universe must either be indifferent to suffering or severely limited in power. Mill says that those who believe in the gospel of salvation and worship God as the creator of the universe have so much to ignore that it can be done only by sophistication and perversion. The Christian moralist is forced to engage in fallacious logic or to draw conclusions that are morally repugnant. 'It may almost always be said, both of sects and individuals, who derive their morality from religion, that the better logicians they are, the worse moralists' ('Utility of Religion', 425). So, although it is possible to say that utilitarianism is a religious doctrine if one assumes that God is a finite being struggling to bring about cosmic happiness, that is not the spirit of the objection. If God is conceived as the Creator of the universe and the director of its course of events, then utilitarianism is profoundly anti-religious. In fact, Mill was sympathetic with the proposal of Auguste Comte, a contemporary French correspondent, that a religion of humanity replace traditional supernatural religion. He thought it would be beneficial if the religious feelings now directed towards worship of a supernatural being were redirected to an ideal of humanity and to humanitarian concerns.

II, 23

Another objection that Mill addresses is that Utility has been stigmatized as an immoral doctrine by giving it the name of Expediency, to contrast it with Principle. To meet this objection, Mill attempts to clarify what is usually meant by the Expedient, when it is opposed to the Right. Elsewhere, Mill uses the term 'expedient' to mean whatever has good consequences, not only what is required by morality but what goes beyond the morally required. He uses it that way in chapter 5. Here he is using it in a narrower derogatory sense. In this sense it generally means that which is useful for the particular interest of the agent himself but contrary to the general welfare, or it means what is useful for some immediate object, some temporary purpose, but which violates a rule whose observance is expedient, i.e., has good consequences when generally observed. Here Mill gives the example of telling a lie to avoid some momentary embarrassment.

But inasmuch as the cultivation in ourselves of a sensitive feeling on the subject of veracity, is one of the most useful, and the enfeeblement of that feeling one of the most hurtful, things to which our conduct can be instrumental; and inasmuch as any, even unintentional, deviation from the truth, does that much towards weakening the trustworthiness of human assertion, which is not only the principal support of all present social well-being, but the insufficiency of which does more than any one thing that can be named to keep back civilization, virtue, everything on which human happiness on the largest scale depends; we feel that the violation, for a present advantage, of a rule of such transcendant expediency, is not expedient, and that he who, for the sake of a convenience to himself or to some other individual, does what depends on him to deprive mankind of the good, and inflict upon them the evil, involved in the greater or less reliance which they can place in each other's word, acts the part of one of their worst enemies. (223 [II, 23])

Here we see not only Mill's praise of the practice of truthfulness and condemnation of lying. We see that for Mill there is seldom a basis for the distinction between act-utilitarianism and rule-utilitarianism: an act in accord with a useful rule strengthens the useful habit of following the rule, and an act in violation of a useful rule weakens the useful habit of following the rule. Furthermore, an act in accord with a useful rule strengthens the social practice of the rule, and an act in violation of a useful rule weakens the social practice of the rule.

Those who argue that the two versions of utilitarianism do not collapse into each other for these reasons can point out that one single act of lying is not going noticeably to affect the social practice of truth-telling – that would require a sizable collection of lies, so act-utilitarianism could justify acts of lying when the act in the particular case has marginally better consequences than telling the truth. If the individual lie were part of a collection of lies that did undermine confidence in veracity, how would one assign consequences to the individual lie? Mill says elsewhere: 'If a hundred infringements would produce all the mischief implied in the abrogation of the rule, a hundredth part of the mischief must be debited to each of the infringements, though we may not be able to trace it home individually. And this hundredth part will generally far outweigh any good expected to arise from the individual act' (Mill 1852: 182).

This notion of 'contributory causation' is controversial, for what if one hundred lies are enough to cause a measurable loss of confidence in veracity, but there are a thousand lies. Is each of the thousand lies to be attributed one thousandth part of the damage, or one hundredth part of the damage. Either distribution has problems. If it is one thousandth, then it will probably not outweigh the good expected to arise from the individual act. If it is a hundredth, then an act whose good in the individual case would outweigh its contribution to the damage would be ruled out. These problems of distributing the consequences of a collection of acts are beside the point if the individual act is not part of a collection of acts. What if it is a rare act that is not accompanied by other acts of violating the rule? The act-utilitarian would then seem be able to say that it is permissible. But Mill elsewhere has an argument against that: 'If one person may break through the rule on his own judgment, the same liberty cannot be refused to others' (ibid.). Mill's conception of morality is sufficiently social that he would not permit agents to be moral 'free-riders'. An individual agent is not permitted to benefit from the security of laws and moral rules and not follow them himself. Mill considers, as an example, the murder of someone whose cruel behaviour tends to increase human unhappiness. The individual act has consequences that favour it, but the counter-consideration on the principle of utility is 'that unless persons were punished for killing, and taught not to kill; that if it were thought allowable for any one to put to death at pleasure any human being whom he believes that the world would be well rid of, nobody's life would be safe' (ibid.). For Mill, an agent is not permitted to maximize utility by engaging in exceptions to useful moral rules unless the exception can be generalized. Mill is not thinking of morality just from the first-person point of view, asking 'What ought I to do?' with the behaviour of others treated as if it were merely one among the circumstances of action. He is thinking of morality from the social point of view, asking 'What morality ought there to be?'

However, Mill says, a rule, such as the rule not to lie, admits of possible exceptions, such as to withhold some fact from a person intent on evil or from a person dangerously ill, when the withholding can only be effected by telling a lie. 'But in order that the exception may not extend itself beyond the need, and may have the least possible effect in weakening reliance on veracity, it ought to be recognized and, if possible, its limits defined . . .' (223 [II, 23]). Thus 'exceptions' can usually be treated not as exceptions but as conformity to a more complex rule allowing those deviations from the simpler rule. To the extent that this can be done, Mill can be interpreted as a thoroughgoing rule-utilitarian. To the extent, however, that he allows utilitarianism to 'temper the rigidity of its laws, by giving a certain latitude, under the moral responsibility of the agent, for accommodation to peculiarities of circumstances . . .' (225 [II, 25]), Mill may be regarded as holding a theory that includes act-utilitarian reasoning and action among its requirements.

II, 24

Another objection that Mill addresses is that there is not time, previous to action, for calculating and weighing the effects of any line of conduct on the general happiness. His answer is 'that there has been ample time, namely, the whole past duration of the human species. During all that time mankind have been learning by experience the tendencies of actions; on which experience all the prudence, as well as all the morality of life, is dependent' (224 [II, 25]). Mill's point is that we already know, in general, what kinds of actions are helpful and harmful. This information is the foundation for the rules of morality. Mill says that by this time mankind must 'have acquired positive beliefs as to the effects of some actions on their happiness; and the beliefs which have thus come down are the rules of morality for the multitude, and for the philosopher until he has succeeded in finding better' (ibid.).

What if philosophers think that they have found a better rule? If it is a rule that does not involve harm to another person, such as the practice of equality in marriage when the multitude believe that a wife should be subservient to her husband and stay at home even if she has talents whose use in a social role would be beneficial, the philosophers can practise the superior rule and hope that others will follow their example, as John Stuart Mill and Harriet Taylor felt about their marriage. Suppose that it does involve some pain to others, as the Mill–Taylor relationship probably involved pain for Mr Taylor during his lifetime. They may believe that the better model of relationships outweighs the pain. But suppose that the rule that the philosophers have found is so controversial as to be currently unlawful. An example would be euthanasia. Many philosophers, as well as other people, believe that ending the life of a terminally ill patient who is in pain and wishes to die would be a better rule than prolonging the dying process through keeping the patient alive. The philosophers may advocate legislative changes to make euthanasia lawful, with legal safeguards so that the practice not be abused. Should the convinced advocate of euthanasia practise it while it is still a criminal act? This is more difficult, for it is breaking two rules – one prohibiting euthanasia, and another more general one that we ought to obey properly enacted laws. Furthermore, there are three ways of engaging in such law-breaking. One is to do it openly and publicly and to take the consequences if prosecuted, hoping that by one's action one can call attention to a bad law. A second is to engage in euthanasia as conformity to a better rule, although an illegal one, as the practice of a rule having better consequences than the one currently recognized, but to do it as quietly as possible in hopes that it will not be noticed. A third is to bring about the desired result with a degree of deceit, such as by the prescription of pain-killers that have the secondary effect of shortening the life of the patient. In situations such as this, there are so many complicating factors that act-utilitarian reasoning is probably required. In some situations one of these would be justified; in others, another. Mill cannot give general instructions on what to do if philosophers have found better rules than are currently being practised. But he does insist that the received code of ethics admits of improvement: 'mankind have still much to learn as to the effects of actions on the general happiness, I admit, or rather, earnestly maintain. The corollaries from the principle of utility, like the precepts of every practical art, admit of indefinite improvement, and, in a progressive state of the human mind, their improvement is perpetually going on' (ibid.).

Mill says that to consider the rules of morality as improvable is one thing; to pass over them entirely and endeavour to test each individual action directly by the first principle of utility is another. Here he is rejecting act-utilitarianism in favour of rule-utilitarianism. He compares the rules to the Nautical Almanack. 'No one argues that the art of navigation is not founded on astronomy, because sailors cannot wait to calculate the Nautical Almanack. Being rational creatures, they go to sea with it ready calculated; and all rational creatures go out upon the sea of life with their minds made up on the common questions of right and wrong ...' (225 [II, 24]).

II, 25

A final objection that Mill considers is the claim that a utilitarian will be apt to make his own particular case an exception to moral rules, and when under temptation will see a utility in the breach of a rule greater than he will see in its observance. Mill's reply is that every moral creed furnishes excuses for evildoing and means of rationalizing behaviour contrary to our conscience. It is not the fault of any creed but the complicated nature of human affairs that rules of conduct cannot be so framed as to require no exceptions, and in the opening thus made, self-deception and dishonest deviancy get in. 'There is no ethical creed which does not temper the rigidity of its laws, by giving a certain latitude, under the moral responsibility of the agent, for accommodation to peculiarities of circumstances ... There exists no moral system under which there do not arise unequivocal cases of conflicting obligation' (225 [II, 25]).

Mill claims that utilitarianism has the advantage in dealing with them, for it possesses an ultimate standard to which conflicting rights and duties can be referred. In other systems, the moral laws all claiming independent authority, there is no common umpire entitled to decide between them, and unless determined by utility, as they commonly are, the conflicts provide scope for personal desires and partialities. Utilitarianism has such a common umpire, but it is not simply the act-utilitarian formula. Mill claims, 'There is no case of moral obligation in which some secondary principle is not involved ...' (226 [II, 25]).

Critical discussion points
In chapter 2, Mill has reviewed at least nine objections to utilitarianism, attempting to answer each. In these answers he has revised the Benthamite theory by introducing the notion that pleasures and pains differ in quality as well as intensity and duration, and he has claimed that there are persons qualified by experiences of alternative pleasures and pains to be competent judges as to which are superior and inferior. Thus Mill does not take happiness to be satisfaction of whatever desires one happens to have. He believes

that people can develop their capacities for happiness, and the fullest life is one including such qualitatively superior pleasures. In this chapter, Mill also calls attention to the role of 'secondary principles', corollaries derived from the principle of utility on the basis of past experience of mankind as to what kinds of actions tend to promote happiness and reduce unhappiness. These corollaries are the basis for the rules of morality that are to be followed. Thus Mill seems to be fundamentally a 'rule-utilitarian'. He does, however, recognize that utilitarianism, as with every code of ethics, tempers the rigidity of its laws to give an agent responsibility to accommodate himself to peculiarities of circumstances and in such cases, presumably, act-utilitarian reasoning may appeal to the ultimate principle of utility for guidance in the particular case. He also claims that progress in morality is possible, its precepts and rules admitting of indefinite improvement. Has Mill adequately answered the objections that he discusses? Is he a consistent hedonist, or has he introduced intrinsic values other than happiness and unhappiness? When he says that by happiness he means pleasure and freedom from pain, has he captured all that is meant by happiness? Is Mill's claim that there are qualitatively superior pleasures correct? Can there be competent judges to settle that issue? Is happiness as attainable as Mill hopes by the improvement of education and social conditions? Is it noble to do without happiness when no greater good comes from it? Can the motive of an action be separated from the morality of it? Has Mill adequately answered the objection that utilitarianism renders agents too cold and calculating? Has he answered the objection that utilitarianism is godless? Has he answered the objections that utilitarianism allows agents to violate principles in the name of expediency or that it allows agents to rationalize actions in their own interest? This is a chapter with great detail and a number of issues that are worthy of further thought.

Study questions

Is Mill's claim that there are higher and lower pleasures consistent with hedonism?
Can the motive of an action be separated from the morality of it?
What is the place of rules in ethics?

CHAPTER 3: OF THE ULTIMATE SANCTION OF THE PRINCIPLE OF UTILITY

Overview

In chapter 3, Mill is addressing the question of what motives there are to follow the utilitarian code of morality. He points out that the question arises whenever a person is called upon to *adopt* a standard. Customary morality, which education and opinion have consecrated, presents itself as being *in itself* obligatory, and when one is asked to believe that morality *derives* its obligation from some more general principle the request is paradoxical. Specific rules, such as not to rob or murder, betray or deceive, seem to be more obligatory than promoting the general happiness, which is proposed as their foundation. Mill claims, however, that this paradox is not peculiar to the doctrine of utility but is inherent in every attempt to analyse morality and to show its foundations. Mill's claim in this chapter is that all the same motives that now lead people to obey customary morality or to obey rules based on any other system of morals can lead them to obey utilitarian morality, and that there are additional sources of motivation as well. Mill makes a distinction between 'external' and 'internal' sanctions. The internal is what we know by the name of 'conscience', and it is this that he calls the ultimate sanction of all morality. Mill gives an analysis of this feeling, and he sees no reason why it cannot be cultivated to as great an intensity in connection with the utilitarian morality as with any other. Finally, he argues that with the advance of civilization there is an increasing tendency for each individual to feel a unity with all other people. Even where these social feelings are weaker than selfish feelings, people feel that they are justified and do not want to be without them.

III, 1–2

Mill says that the question is asked of any supposed moral standard, 'What is its sanction?' (227 [III, 1]). In English, the word 'sanction' is ambiguous. One meaning is positive: to sanction something is to authorize or endorse it. But in law and ethics, it means the enforcement of a law or rule by reward or punishment, pleasure or pain, usually emphasizing the negative – punishment or pain. So when he asks the question, 'what is the sanction of the principle of utility', Mill is asking what can motivate one to obey its dictates.

Mill points out that the question 'what is its sanction' arises when a person is called on to recognize a standard at the foundation of morality distinct from the rules not to steal, murder, or lie. The rules supposedly derived from the foundation seem to have more authority than the foundation. Mill says that this will continue to be the case

> until the influences which form moral character have taken the same hold of the principle which they have taken of some of the consequences – until, by the improvement of education, the feeling of unity with our fellow creatures shall be ... as deeply rooted in our character, and to our own consciousness as completely a part of our nature, as the horror of crime is in an ordinarily well-brought up young person. (227 [III, 2])

Mill claims that the difficulty is not unique to utilitarianism but is true of every attempt to analyse morality and reduce it to its principles.

III, 3

Mill claims that the principle of utility has all the sanctions that belong to any other system of morals. Those sanctions are either external or internal. By 'external', Mill is referring to enforcement of morality by external sources of authority; by 'internal' he is referring to the agent's own conscience.

Bentham had analysed sanctions as sources of pleasure and pain that motivate all actions. He listed them as physical, political, popular and religious. By 'physical', he meant the laws of nature that give positive and negative reinforcement to various kinds of behaviour. These are the causal relations in nature by which people learn that certain things give pleasure and others give pain. If one does not eat, one feels the pain of hunger; if one does eat, one feels the pleasure of satisfying one's appetite. That would be an example of a physical sanction. By 'political', Bentham meant the pleasures and pains meted out by judges and other state officials. By 'popular', Bentham meant the pleasures and pains produced in an agent by the response to actions by unofficial persons in the community that one has dealings with. Among these are the approval and disapproval of other people. One tends to feel pleasure when others approve of one's actions, pain, when they disapprove. By 'religious', Bentham referred to pleasures and pains expected to be experienced in this life or a future one bestowed by a superior invisible being.

Mill ignores Bentham's physical sanction as not relevant to morality, and he lumps together the political and popular. He summarizes the external as 'the hope of favour and fear of displeasure from our fellow creatures or from the Ruler of the Universe, along with whatever we may have of sympathy or affection for them, or of love and awe of Him, inclining us to do his will independently of selfish consequences' (228 [III, 3]).

Mill sees no reason why these should not attach themselves to the utilitarian morality as completely and as powerfully as to any other. In fact, men do desire happiness, and they desire and commend all conduct in others towards themselves by which they think their happiness is promoted. And if they believe in the goodness of God, they will necessarily believe that promotion of happiness is what God approves.

III, 4

It is the internal sanction, however, in which Mill is primarily interested. Mill describes this as 'a feeling in our own mind; a pain, more or less intense, attendant on violation of duty, which in properly-cultivated moral natures rises, in the more serious cases, into shrinking from it as an impossibility' (228 [III, 4]). Mill was critical of Bentham's psychology on this point. He says that Bentham held that all actions are determined by pains and pleasures *in prospect*, pains and pleasures to which we look forward as the *consequences* of our acts. Mill believes that this if false.

> The pain or pleasure which determines our conduct is as frequently one which *precedes* the moment of action as one which follows it. A man *may*, it is true, be deterred, in circumstances of temptation, from perpetrating a crime, by his dread of punishment, or of the remorse, which he fears he may have to endure *after* the guilty act ... But the case *may* be, and is to the full as likely to be, that he recoils from the very thought of committing the act; the idea of placing himself in such a situation is so painful, that he cannot dwell upon it long enough to have even the physical power of perpetrating the crime. His conduct is determined by pain; but by a pain which precedes the act, not by

one which is expected to follow it. Not only *may* this be so, but unless it be so, the man is not really virtuous. (Mill 1833: 12)

Mill would also have said that when one is contemplating a virtuous act, one feels pleasure preceding the act. At the end of this chapter, when Mill discusses the feeling of solidarity with other people, the positive feeling of identity of interests with others is as important as repulsion at opposing their interests.

Mill says that this internal sanction is extremely complex. When connected to the pure idea of duty, of doing what one ought to do, it can be called 'conscience', but as it actually exists, 'the simple fact is in general all encrusted over with collateral associations, derived from sympathy, from love, and still more from fear; from all the forms of religious feeling; from the recollections of childhood and of all our past life; from self-esteem, desire of the esteem of others, and occasionally even self-abasement' (228 [III, 4]).

This extreme complication, Mill thinks, is what gives it a sort of mystical character that makes people think that it cannot possibly attach itself to any other objects than those which are found in our present experience to excite it.

III, 5–6
Mill calls this subjective feeling in our own minds – the con-scientious feelings of mankind – the ultimate sanction of all mor-ality, and he sees no reason why it may not be the ultimate motive of utilitarian morality. 'No reason has ever been shown why they may not be cultivated to as great intensity in connexion with the utilitarian, as with any other rule of morals' (229 [III, 5]). It will bind only those in whom the feelings have developed. For those who do not possess the feelings, only the external sanctions will apply. But this is true of any morality, not just the utilitarian.

Is Mill correct here? As we know from chapter 2, the specific rules of utilitarian morality are derived from the principle of utility, whereas for customary or intuitive morality it is the rules them-selves that are felt to be obligatory. Isn't it possible that the feeling of duty is stronger when the duty is seen as a duty not to rob, not to steal, not to lie, rather than not to rob, steal, or lie because these cause general unhappiness? Mill acknowledges that this is true in the present state of morality – 'I feel that I am bound not to rob or murder, betray or deceive; but why am I bound to promote the general happiness?' (225 [III, 1]). There is the *possibility* that a utilitarian morality will be able to induce as strong a sense of duty and conscience as customary or intuitive morality, but is it likely? There are those who say that seeing moral obligation to be an objective reality will make a person more likely to be obedient to it than one who believes it to be entirely subjective. If I say that that which is restraining me is only a feeling in my own mind, I may seek to get rid of it. Mill says that this danger is not confined to utilitarian morality. 'The question, Need I obey my conscience? is quite as often put to themselves by persons who never heard of the principle of utility, as by its adherents' (230 [III, 6]). Again, the question may arise for a non-utilitarian, but for some non-utilitarians there are additional (external) sanctions – hope of favour and fear of other people or of God – that may be stronger than for a utilitarian if they believe that the authority of morality derives from custom or convention or from God, rather than from utility.

III, 7–9

In these paragraphs Mill discusses whether the feeling of duty is innate or acquired. First, if it is innate, Mill sees no reason why the feeling should not be that of regard to the pleasures and pain of others; and intuitive moralists, although they believe that there are other intuitive moral obligations, already believe this to be one of them. They unanimously hold that a large portion of morality turns upon the consideration of the interest of our fellow creatures.

Mill's own belief, however, is that moral feelings are not innate but acquired, although not for that reason any less natural. It is natural to man to speak, to build cities, to cultivate the ground, though these are acquired faculties. Like these, moral feelings are capable of a high degree of development, but also of being cultivated in almost any direction. When recognized as a product of conditioning or, in Mill's terminology, 'associations', the feeling of duty, even after it had been implanted by education, might be analysed away, and this could be true of the feeling of duty when associated with utility if there were no natural sentiment to incline us to it and to foster it in others. Mill is here recognizing that philosophical analysis can undermine the acquired moral feelings. But he is also setting up the reader for his concluding paragraphs.

III, 10–11

Mill asserts that there *is* this basis of powerful natural sentiment. This is the social feelings of mankind, the desire to be in unity with our fellow creatures, 'which is already a powerful principle in human nature, and happily one of those which tend to become stronger, even without express inculcation, from the influences of advancing civilization' (231 [III, 10]). Mill claims that everyone is a member of some social body in which the interests of all are to be consulted, and society among equals requires that all be consulted equally. When people co-operate with others, the collective, not an individual, interest is the aim. 'Not only does all strengthening of social ties, and all healthy growth of society, give to each individual a stronger personal interest in practically consulting the welfare of others; it also leads him to identify his *feelings* more and more with their good, or at least with an ever greater degree of practical consideration for it' (ibid.). Mill envisions that, as civilization goes on, this will be felt to be more and more natural.

> Every step in political improvement renders it more so, by removing the sources of opposition of interest, and levelling those inequalities of legal privilege between individuals or classes, owing to which there are large portions of mankind whose happiness it is still practicable to disregard. In an improving state of the human mind, the influences are constantly on the increase, which tend to generate in each individual a feeling of unity with all the rest. (232 [III, 10])

If we suppose this feeling of unity to be taught as a religion, with the whole force of education, of institutions and of opinion, directed to make everyone from infancy surrounded by the profession and by the practice of it, Mill thinks that no one would have doubts about the sufficiency of the ultimate sanction for the morality of happiness. He refers to Auguste Comte (1798–1857), French sociologist and philosopher, who proposed such a religion of humanity. Mill says that Comte has shown the possibility of giving to the service of humanity, even without the aid of belief in Providence, both the psychical power and the social efficacy of a religion. But Mill also states his reservation that in Comte's details of the proposal, it would be so excessive as to interfere unduly with human freedom and individuality.

Even in the present state of society, Mill says, every individual even now tends to feel that there should be harmony between his feelings and aims and those of his fellow creatures. This feeling in most individuals is much inferior in strength to their selfish feelings, but to those who have it it has the character of a natural feeling. 'It does not present itself to their minds as a superstition of education, or a law despotically imposed by the power of society, but as an attribute which it would not be well for them to be without. This conviction is the ultimate sanction of the greatest-happiness morality' (233 [III, 11]). It constitutes in itself a powerful internal binding force.

In chapter 3, Mill is doing moral psychology. He is first attempting to show what motivates anyone has to be moral, regardless of the content of the moral principles. These are the external and internal sanctions that he describes. He then argues that there is an additional source of motivation for utilitarian morality. Mill's psychological theory is called 'associationism'. Mill did not write a self-contained psychology book, but he wrote notes to a second edition of his father's *Analysis of the Phenomena of the Human Mind*. J. S. Mill's notes are as extensive as the original text. In this book James Mill gives an associationist account of much motivation, including moral motivation. He thinks that there is a universal feeling of sympathy for the happiness or suffering of other individuals. When we see others enjoying pleasure, it gives us pleasure; when we see others in pain, it gives us pain. As our complex idea of mankind is made up of the aggregate of ideas of individuals, through pleasure associated with their pleasures and pain associated with their pains, we can come to have a general desire for the happiness of mankind and a general aversion for the unhappiness of mankind. Through the multitude and variety of the pleasurable ideas associated with other people, it is possible that the moral sentiments may be formed and, in their maturity, be perfectly disinterested. J. S. Mill agrees with this much of his father's psychology.

However, J. S. Mill differs from Bentham and James Mill in calling attention to the fact that a course of action that was originally willed because it was associated with pleasure or avoidance of pain may be willed out of habit. 'As we proceed in the formation of habits, and become accustomed to will a particular act or a particular course of conduct because it is pleasurable, we at last continue to will it without any reference to its being pleasurable' (Mill 1843: 842 [bk 6, ch 2, § 4]). At this stage we have a 'person of confirmed virtue' who 'carries out his purposes without any thought of the pleasure he has in contemplating them or expects to derive from their fulfillment; and persists in acting on them, even though these pleasures are much diminished ... or are outweighed by the pains which the pursuit of the purposes may bring upon him' (238 [IV, 11]). In this way Mill can account for the hero and the martyr who voluntarily do without happiness for the sake of something that they prize more than their *individual* happiness. And he can better account for the disinterested utilitarian virtue of promoting the general happiness. One can come to associate one's own happiness with the happiness of others, coming to desire the happiness of others as a part of one's own happiness, and one can develop a confirmed character of acting to promote the interest of others. Not all actions that were *originally* motivated by one's own pleasure and avoidance of pain need to be motivated, after one has become a person of confirmed character, by one's own pleasure and avoidance of pain on the occasion of acting.

Critical discussion points
In this chapter, Mill has analysed the subjective feeling of conscience – to do one's duty – and he sees no reason why it cannot be as binding when attached to utilitarian morality as to any other. In fact, he concludes that with the advance of social equality and co-operation, there is a natural basis for the impartiality of utilitarianism. There are a number of questions to be raised about Mill's discussion. Mill calls the subjective feeling of conscience the ultimate sanction of morality, but is it 'ultimate' or is it merely a subjective internalization of the external sanctions which are the ultimate sanction of morality? Mill recognizes that some people do not have these moral feelings, yet morality can be enforced upon them by law or by opinion. Perhaps law and opinion are the *ultimate* sanctions of morality. Another question is whether Mill is correct that this feeling is acquired, rather than innate and, if innate, that it would attach to the utilitarian concern for general happiness. If innate, perhaps to have had survival value it would have attached to more limited loyalties, such as the welfare of family, clan, tribe, or friends, rather than to the general welfare of all. Or the survival value might have been to be repulsed by specific

acts such as incest, or killing a member of one's clan, or lying to a family member or friend. If acquired, as Mill supposes, can it be directed to the general happiness, as Mill claims? Mill's moral psychology rests upon a controversial theory of association or conditioning. Is that theory sound?

Mill recognizes that there are conflicts of interest between people in the wretched social conditions in which he lives, but he envisions progress towards a condition of greater equality and co-operation. Is this likely to occur? What are some of the obstacles in the way? Capitalism as an economic system is based on self-interest. Nation states give privileges to their citizens, setting up laws against unlimited immigration. Religions and sects within religions fight with one other. Do we see evidence of the sort of growing interdependence of interests and equality that Mill believes is characteristic of advancing 'civilization'?

Study questions

Is conscience the ultimate sanction of morality or is the ultimate sanction law and opinion?

Can the sanctions of morality be applied to utilitarianism as easily as to a morality consisting of accepted rules?

Is there evidence that advancing civilization is making people identify their interests with one another?

CHAPTER 4: OF WHAT SORT OF PROOF THE PRINCIPLE OF UTILITY IS SUSCEPTIBLE

Overview

Every version of utilitarianism requires an account of what are good and bad consequences. Mill's account is that happiness and unhappiness are the criteria of good and bad consequences as ends, all other values deriving their value as means to happiness or the prevention of unhappiness, or as 'parts' of happiness and unhappiness. In this chapter, Mill lays out what sort of proof can be given to support this position. He says that it is not proof in the ordinary use of the term, but at the end of the chapter he says that if his account is true, the principle of utility – that happiness alone is good as an end – is proved. His argument is based on the psychology of what people desire as ends. In the details of his argument, Mill has been accused by interpreters of committing a number of logical fallacies. Mill was the author of a textbook in logic. Isn't it more likely that he is being misinterpreted than that he is committing logical bloopers? But Mill does say things that can be misleading to a twenty-first century reader. These require explanation to be understood. The proof has not been accepted as sound by many scholars. In conclusion, an outline of the proof indicating its most controversial features will be presented.

I, 1–3

'The utilitarian doctrine is', Mill says, 'that happiness is desirable, and the only thing desirable, as an end; all other things being only desirable as means to that end' (234 [IV, 2]). How can this make good its claim to be believed? Mill says that to be incapable of proof by reasoning is common to all first principles, those of knowledge as well as those of conduct. But the former, being matters of fact, can be subject to a direct appeal to the senses. Mill claims that what people actually desire is that to which appeal can be made as to what is desirable. 'The only proof capable of being given that an object is visible, is that people actually see it. The only proof that a sound is audible, is that people hear it: and so of the other sources of our experience. In like manner, I apprehend, the sole evidence it is possible to produce that anything is desirable, is that people do actually desire it' (234 [IV, 3]).

Some interpreters have taken this comparison of 'desirable' to 'visible' literally and accused Mill of an error here. They say that 'visible' means 'capable of being seen', while desirable means 'worthy of being desired', not 'capable of being desired'. But Mill has explicitly said that he is attempting to prove a first principle of conduct, not a matter of fact. If he meant by desirable 'capable of being desired', that would be a matter of fact. So that is not how Mill should be interpreted.

The comparison of desirable to visible and audible is not to make an exact parallel between the senses and the desiring faculty, but to claim that there is evidence that can be appealed to in both cases. The evidence that something is visible is that it is seen. The evidence that something is desirable is that it is desired. If happiness were not actually desired, no one would be convinced that it is desirable. But it is desired: 'each person, so far as he believes it to be attainable, desires his own happiness. This, however, being a fact, we have not only all the proof which the case admits of, but all which it is possible to require, that happiness is a good: that each person's happiness is a good to that person, and the general happiness, therefore, a good to the aggregate of all persons' (ibid.).

Notice that Mill moves from the claim that happiness is a good to each person, based on each person's desire for his own happiness, to the claim that the general happiness is a good to the aggregate of all persons. Here Mill has been accused of committing the 'fallacy of composition' – claiming that what is true of a part is true of a whole. An example of this would be saying that because each grain of sand is small, therefore an aggregate of a million grains is small. Is that the character of Mill's argument? Mill was asked about this argument and his reply is in a letter to a correspondent:

As to the sentence you quote from my *Utilitarianism*, when I said that the general happiness is a good to the aggregate of all persons I did not mean that every human being's happiness is a good to every other human being, though I think in a good state of society and education it would be so. I merely meant in this particular sentence to argue that since A's happiness is a good, B's a good, C's a good, etc., the sum of all these goods must be a good. (Mill 1868: 1414)

Mill is claiming that if we ask what is good for A, B and C, at least part of it is A's happiness plus B's happiness plus C's happiness. This is indeed a controversial claim, but Mill thinks that it is uncontroversial. He evidently thinks that the evidence of desire, showing that each person desires his own happiness, shows that happiness is the *kind* of thing that is desirable and each person's happiness adds to the general happiness. He thinks that happiness has been shown to be *objectively* good, not that each person thinks merely subjectively that it is good for him. He also thinks that instances of happiness can be added together to get a sum of happiness, and therefore individual 'goods' can be added together to get a sum of goods. Regarding it in this light, he can say, in a footnote in chapter 5,

equal amounts of happiness are equally desirable whether felt by the same or by different persons. This, however, is not a pre-supposition; not a premise needful to support the principle of utility, but the very principle itself ... If there is any anterior principle implied, it can be no other than this, that the truths of arithmetic are applicable to the valuation of happiness, as of all other measurable quantities. (257–8 [V, 36])

IV, 4–8

Mill thinks that each person's desire for his own happiness has shown that happiness is *one* of the ends of conduct, and consequently one of the criteria of morality, but it has not proved itself to be the sole criterion. To do that it would seem necessary to show that people never desire anything other than happiness, but it is obvious 'that they do desire things which, in common language, are decidedly distinguished from happiness. They desire, for example, virtue, and the absence of vice, no less really than pleasure and absence of pain' (235 [IV, 4]). How does Mill answer this objection that the evidence of desire indicates that there are things other than happiness that are desired? He claims that this is not contrary to his principle:

> The ingredients of happiness are very various, and each of them is desirable in itself, and not merely when considered as swelling an aggregate. The principle of utility does not mean that any given pleasure, as music, for instance, or any given exemption from pain, as for example health, are to be looked upon as means to a collective something termed happiness, and to be desired on that account. They are desired and desirable in and for themselves; besides being means, they are a part of the end. (235 [IV, 5])

Isn't Mill being confusing here? Isn't he admitting that happiness is not the only thing desired as an end, but that virtue, music and health are all desired in themselves? And, if so, why has he not admitted that it is false that happiness is the only thing desirable as an end?

Mill's position becomes somewhat clearer and more convincing when we remember that he holds an associationist psychology. 'Virtue, according to the utilitarian doctrine, is not naturally and originally part of the end, but it is capable of becoming so; and in those who love it disinterestedly it has become so, and is desired and cherished, not as a means to happiness, but as a part of their happiness' (ibid.). So Mill's theory of how virtue comes to be desired as an end is that it is through association with pleasure, and association of pain with vice. Pleasure and pain are the original sources of motivation, the original causes of desires and aversions, but through association or conditioning, the desires and aversions come to be for pleasure and pain *derived from virtue and vice*, not simply for pure pleasure and pain.

Mill points out that virtue is not the only thing, originally a means, which by association comes to be desired for itself. Love of money is another example. There is originally no desire for money but for what it will buy, but it can come to be desired in and for itself, and the desire to possess it may be stronger than the desire to use it. 'It may be then said truly, that money is desired not for the sake of an end, but as part of the end. From being a means to happiness, it has come to be itself a principal ingredient of the individual's conception of happiness' (236 [IV, 6]).

Other examples are power and fame. It is the strong association generated between them and other objects of desire that gives them the intensity in some people to surpass in strength all other desires.

In these cases the means have become a part of the end, and a more important part of it than any of the things which they are means to. What was once desired as an instrument for the attainment of happiness, has come to be desired for its own sake. In being desired for its own sake it is, however, desired as *part* of happiness. The person is made, or thinks he would be made, happy by its mere possession; and is made unhappy by failure to obtain it. The desire of it is not a different thing from the desire of happiness, any more than the love of music, or the desire of health. They are included in happiness. They are some of the elements of which the desire of happiness is made up. Happiness is not an abstract idea, but a concrete whole; and these are some of its parts. (ibid.)

So Mill is claiming the priority of pleasure and pain in time – the person desires pleasure as an end before virtue or money or power or fame comes to be desired as an end – and pleasure and pain are necessary conditions for the desire of these other things.

Those who desire virtue for its own sake, desire it either because the consciousness of it is a pleasure, or because the consciousness of being without it is a pain, or for both reasons united; as in truth the pleasure and pain seldom exist separately, but almost always together, the same person feeling pleasure in the degree of virtue attained, and pain in not having attained more. If one of these gave him no pleasure, and the other no pain, he would not love or desire virtue, or would desire it only for the other benefits which it might produce to himself or to persons whom he cared for. (237 [IV, 8])

IV, 9

Mill concludes that the psychological argument just given answers the question of the proof to which the principle of utility is susceptible. 'If the opinion which I have now stated is psychologically true – if human nature is so constituted as to desire nothing which is not either a part of happiness or a means of happiness, we can have no other proof, and we require no other, that these are the only things desirable' (237 [IV, 9]).

He asserts that happiness is the sole end of human action, and the promotion of it is the test by which to judge all human conduct; 'from whence it necessarily follows that it must be the criterion of morality, since a part is included in the whole' (ibid.).

Remember that morality for Mill is only one department of the 'Art of Life' that includes other practical ends, but he thinks that his psychological argument encompasses all of these – happiness is the value to be sought in all departments. In chapter 5, we shall see how he distinguishes morality from the other departments. In paragraph 11, we shall see that there are other ends of human action, namely those arising from habit. So Mill should have said here that happiness is the sole end of *consciously desired* human action.

IV, 10

Mill reminds us that this argument is based upon evidence. It can only be determined by 'practised self-consciousness and self-observation, assisted by observation of others' (237 [IV, 10]). He believes that these sources of evidence will declare

that desiring a thing and finding it pleasant, aversion to it and thinking of it as painful, are phenomena entirely inseparable, or rather two parts of the same phenomenon; in strictness of language, two different modes of naming the same psychological fact: that to think of an object as desirable (unless for the sake of its consequences), and to think of it as pleasant, are one and the same thing; and that to desire anything, except in proportion as the idea of it is pleasant, is a physical and metaphysical impossibility. (237–8 [IV, 10])

The use of the term 'metaphysical' here is disconcerting to a twenty-first-century reader. It has come to have a specialized meaning in philosophy different from the use in the nineteenth century, where it was synonymous with 'psychological'. This paragraph has also been interpreted by commentators to claim that Mill is *defining* happiness as that which is desired as an end. But Mill is not making a linguistic claim. He is making a factual claim. He asks the reader to engage in self-consciousness and self-observation. That would not be relevant if he were *defining* happiness as that which is desired as an end.

IV, 11–12
An objection can be made that pleasure and exception from pain are not the sole motivating forces of human action. People do many things without thinking about what they are doing and without feeling any pleasure or pain either at the time of the action or as an expectation of the action. Mill recognizes this: 'a person of confirmed virtue, or any person whose purposes are fixed, carries out his purposes without any thought of the pleasure he has in contemplating them, or expects to derive from their fulfillment ...' (238 [IV, 11]). Mill answers this by making a distinction between will and desire. Will is different from desire and though originally based on desire, it may take on a life of its own: 'in the case of an habitual purpose, instead of willing the thing because we desire it, we often desire it only because we will it' (ibid.). This is the familiar power of habit. Sometimes a thing is done unconsciously, the consciousness coming only after the action. Sometimes the action is conscious and even in opposition to deliberate preference. 'It is not the less true that will, in the beginning, is entirely produced by desire ... Will is the child of desire, and passes out of the dominion of its parent only to come under that of habit. That which is the result of habit affords no presumption of being intrinsically good ...' (238–9 [IV, 11]). An example of this habit formation would be obsessive or addictive

behaviour that is even contrary to conscious desire, or any pattern of behaviour that has become habitual and is done without thought or deliberations. Mill's claim, then, leaves him with everything that affords any presumption of being intrinsically good being also an object of conscious desire. But in feeling and in conduct, Mill says, will imparts certainty; so the will to do *right* ought to be cultivated into habitual independence. In that case the will is a means to good, not intrinsically a good; and this 'does not contradict the doctrine that nothing is a good to human beings but in so far as it is either itself pleasurable, or a means of attaining pleasure or averting pain' (239 [IV, 11]).

And so Mill concludes: 'if this doctrine be true, the principle of utility is proved. Whether it is so or not, must now be left to the consideration of the thoughtful reader' (239 [IV, 12]).

Critical discussion points

Mill says that the sort of proof that the principle of utility is susceptible of is not proof in the ordinary sense of the term, but it is a logical argument based on premises. If we see it in that form, we can detect the more controversial steps in the argument. Much of it can be stated in Mill's own words.

(1) 'The sole evidence it is possible to produce that anything is desirable is that people do actually desire it' (para. 3).
(2) 'Each person, so far as he believes it to be attainable, desires his own happiness' (para. 3). Therefore,
(3) 'Happiness is a good' (para. 3). Mill substitutes 'is a good' for 'is desirable', but I think that this is only to avoid repetition. In this context he regards these expressions as interchangeable.
(4) Each person desires nothing that is not either a part of his happiness or a means to his happiness. Mill's exact words are: 'Human nature is so constituted as to desire nothing which is not either a part of happiness or a means to happiness' (para. 9, but argued through paras. 5–10). Therefore,
(5) '...[H]appiness is desirable, as an end, all other things being only desirable as means to that end' (para. 2) – the utilitarian doctrine.

This is the simple outline of the argument. It is made more complicated by the fact that each individual's desire is for his own happiness, whereas the utilitarian doctrine that Mill wishes to establish is that the *general* happiness is the foundation of morality. This is explicit in paragraph 3 where he says: '... each person's happiness is a good to that person, and the general happiness, therefore, a good to the aggregate of all persons'. To make the second half of the argument parallel, he would have to say: 'Each person desires nothing that is not either a part of his happiness or a means to his happiness, therefore happiness is desirable as an end, all other things being only desirable as means to that end, for each person; and the general happiness is desirable as an end, all other things being only desirable as means to that end, for the aggregate of all persons'.

When put in this form, we see that (1) is a methodological premise; (2) and (4) are psychological premises; and there is the deduction of (3) and (5) from (2) and (4). (2) is probably uncontroversial. One's own happiness, even interpreted as 'an existence made up of few and transitory pains, many and various pleasures' (215 [II, 11]) is at least one thing desired as an end by each person. Even an ascetic desires happiness, but he may believe that it is attainable only in an afterlife or by means of enduring physical pain. The controversial premises are (1), (4) and the move from each person's happiness being a good for that person to the conclusion that the general happiness is a good and the only good for the aggregate of all persons. A further point of controversy might be Mill's effort to make morality one department of the Art of Life, but that will be discussed in more detail in reading chapter 5.

Is actual desire the sole evidence it is possible to produce that anything is desirable? It is hardly necessary to point out that Mill is not saying that 'desirable' or 'good' *means* 'desired'. But Mill leaves himself open to this charge by his language in a footnote in chapter 5, where he says, 'for what is the principle of utility, if it be not that "happiness" and "desirable" are synonymous terms' (257n [V, 36]). This is a puzzling use of 'synonymous', but it would be absurd to think that Mill's appeal to psychological evidence, 'practiced self-consciousness and self-observation, assisted by the observation of others' (237 [IV, 10]), is to support the claim that the word 'happiness' simply *means* 'desirable'. Mill apparently means that the two terms refer to the same psychological phenomena, one descriptively, the other normatively. Mill is quite explicit in distinguishing factual from normative propositions. Mill is appealing to the psychological fact of desire to support the normative claim as to what is to be sought, of what is good, of what ends are worth pursuing. To say that they refer to the same thing is the conclusion of his argument, not the starting point.

What might be alternatives to desire as evidence for what is desirable? Mill does not address the claim by the ancient Greek philosopher Aristotle (384–322 BC) that rational activity is what constitutes the good for human beings. Aristotle based this on a normative theory of nature – that every faculty has some purpose, and that the unique faculty that humans have – that plants and other animals do not have – is rationality. Mill would probably argue that rationality has survival value – he was an admirer of Darwin's theory of evolution – and is thus a means to the end, not the end. Furthermore, Aristotle's strongest arguments against hedonism in the final book of his *Nicomachean Ethics* are based on the evidence of desire. Aristotle says that we would like to possess various capacities and engage in various activities even if they brought no pleasure, such as seeing, remembering, knowing and being virtuous. Pleasures do accompany these, but he says that we would want them even if no pleasure resulted. This is a challenge to Mill's claim that we would not desire them as ends but only as means if they were not part of our happiness, but Aristotle here, like Mill, is appealing to the evidence of desire. Those who reject Mill's appeal to the evidence of desire have the burden of proof to say what other evidence there is. As indicated in discussing chapter 1, Mill has arguments against intuitionism, the appeal to Nature and the appeal to divine command. Is there any other alternative to the evidence of desire?

The controversial psychological fact that Mill is arguing for in this chapter is that people desire nothing as ends unless they are parts of their happiness. Mill does not use the term, but I think that we can call his view a form of 'psychological hedonism' – that pleasure and pain are the only motives for human action – with two complications: that pleasure and pain may have been the original sources of motivation but that through association, although still motivating, it is no longer the focus of attention in what one consciously desires; and, secondly, that behaviour may become habitual to the point that there is no pleasure or freedom from pain found in the actions. Is this theory psychologically true, and has Mill analysed the psychological phenomena accurately? What about Aristotle's claim that we would desire seeing, remembering, knowing and being virtuous, even if these brought no pleasure? This is a difficult question because they *do* bring pleasure or, at least, avoidance of pain. If one is blind, there are no visual pleasures, and there are inconveniences in not being able to see. If one cannot remember, one is hardly a person, with no knowledge of friends and loved ones; and memories are for the most part pleasurable. But what if they are not? Do you still want to remember things that bring you pain? Knowledge is generally useful, and its absence a source of error and pain. But if knowledge is painful – and not useful – do you want to have it anyway? Out of habit, you may say that you want to know, but isn't that from the fact that you want the freedom to decide on the basis of the knowledge whether or not it is useful. If it turns out to be useless and painful, aren't you willing to say that you had rather not known?

In addition to Aristotle's candidates for intrinsic value, there is the claim that loving relationships are valuable apart from the pleasure that they give. Under normal circumstances, they do give pleasure, but what if the love requires sacrifice or turns into loss or hate. Is it always better to have loved and lost than never to have loved at all? And, if so, is it the love by itself that was valuable, or the joy of the love that is worth the pain of the loss? Much dramatic tragedy is based upon the pain of love, and it is a difficult question whether love that in the end is painful is such that its worth is more than the pleasure of the love. I leave the reader to reflect upon that.

Other versions of utilitarianism are not restricted to pleasure and pain as values as ends. Some utilitarians go beyond hedonism in their list of intrinsic values, counting such things as achievement, knowledge and love as ends, based – as Mill bases them – on the objects of desire. These are not challenges to Mill's methodology of appeal to desire as the basis for judgement, but are challenges to his psychological analysis. Is his psychological analysis accurate? Can these other objects of desire be analysed as 'parts' of happiness, as Mill does, or are they independent objects of desire?

Having established what is a good for each individual, whether it be pleasure and freedom from pain, as Mill claims, or some richer list of intrinsic goods, as some other utilitarians have claimed, Mill generalizes this to the general good for the aggregate of all individuals. Critics have often attributed more to Mill than is warranted. Mill is not saying that the aggregate of all individuals is a collective body that has its own interests independent of the interests of the individuals who make up the aggregate. And he is not imposing an equalitarian doctrine that the general good must be distributed in any particular way, except to say that equal amounts of the good are to be counted equally. At this stage of the argument, he is simply saying that the evidence of desire determines that, for each individual, happiness is the common denominator of what is desired. Happiness is a necessary and sufficient condition for something to be desired as an end. If that is true, he argues, then it is a necessary and sufficient condition for the good of each member of an aggregate. He regards the aggregate as simply the numeration of the individuals who make up the group, and he regards the good for those individuals as simply the summation of the good for each added together.

It might be claimed that happiness is not something that can be added between different individuals. Why not? If I have a certain amount of happiness, and you have a certain amount of happiness, don't the two of us together have twice the happiness of each one individually? It is not that if I had your happiness in addition to mine, I would be twice as happy: that is more difficult to conceptualize. But, Mill is claiming, happiness is something quantifiable, even if we don't have a hedonic thermometer to measure it. And even with the complexity of quality of happiness, it has a degree that can exceed a lesser degree. To deny Mill's generalization that a summation of individuals' happiness equals the general happiness, one has to claim that happiness is not an objective psychological state. Even if the happiness is not the greatest happiness that one can obtain because of inexperience of alternatives, a present state of happiness is an objective psychological fact, isn't it? To say that it is all in the mind of the person having the experience is not to deny that it is a fact in the mind of that person, with quantitative and qualitative dimensions. Mill's conclusion is not uncontroversial, but it is plausible. If you wish to benefit three friends, A, B and C, by making them happy, don't you regard the sum of the happiness of all three as an objective to be obtained?

In conclusion, Mill's 'proof' is not such that denial of it involves a contradiction. The appeal to desire as the evidence of desire is controversial. The claim that no one desires anything as an end unless it is a part of happiness, and that such desire is evidence that happiness is what makes anything valuable as an end, is controversial. And the claim that what is good for each individual in an aggregate can be summed up to give what is generally good for all individuals in the group is subject to criticism. But those who do not accept his proof have to disprove it. What evidence or arguments can be given against it?

Study questions

Is actual desire the sole evidence of what is desirable?
Do people desire nothing as an end unless it is part of their conception of happiness?
Is what is good for an aggregate of persons the sum of what is good for the individuals in the aggregate?

CHAPTER 5: ON THE CONNEXION BETWEEN JUSTICE AND UTILITY

Overview

One of the chief objections to utilitarianism, in all its forms, is that it is sometimes in conflict with the demands of justice. Utilitarianism is said to be an aggregative philosophy: the greatest *amount* of happiness, or other intrinsic value, is the criterion of correct action, regardless of the *distribution* of the value. But justice, so the objection goes, requires that values be distributed justly, not only that there is the greatest amount. Theories of justice are sometimes classified as 'penal' or 'retributive', having to do with the justice of punishment; and 'distributive', having to do with the distribution of the benefits and burdens of society independent of the punishment of wrongs, such as the justice of wealth and income inequality or of taxation. Mill's analysis of justice is intended to apply to both penal and distributive justice. After his analysis of justice and its sentiment, he discusses the variety of opinions regarding the justice of punishment – penal justice – and the justice of wages and taxation – distributive justice.

In chapter 5, Mill is seeking to answer the objection that justice is in conflict with utility. His procedure is first, by an analysis of the common-sense uses of the terms 'justice' and 'injustice', to find the common characteristics of the concepts before inquiring as to their relationship to utility. Part of this inquiry is to distinguish between the *concepts* of justice and injustice and the *sentiment* attached to instances of justice and injustice – that emotional feeling that people feel when confronted with them. Mill recognizes that the subjective mental feeling, the sentiment, towards instances of justice and injustice is different from that which commonly attaches to the general promotion of happiness and prevention of unhappiness. Mill admits that this sentiment of justice does not arise from the idea of utility, but he argues that what is *moral* in the sentiment does depend upon utility. He claims that justice is a particular kind or branch of general utility, and that there is a utilitarian basis for making the demands of justice more imperative than the demands of other moral obligations. Part of his argument is that if justice is something distinct from utility, which the mind can recognize by simple introspection, it is hard to understand why there is so much controversy over what is just in punishment, in wages and in taxation. There are conflicting opinions about what is just and unjust in these areas, not a single doctrine. If, on the other hand, justice is subordinate to utility, this is explicable. There will be as much difference of opinion about what is just as there is about what is useful to society.

To analyse the concept, Mill goes through six ideas that are associated with what is just or unjust, and then examines the etymology of the word. He concludes that the idea of penal sanction is the generating idea of the notion of justice, but that does not distinguish it from moral obligation in general. To make that distinction, Mill appeals to the difference between those duties in which a correlative *right* resides in some person or persons, and those moral obligations that do not give birth to any right. He then analyses what it is to have a right. When asked why society ought to recognize rights, he says that he can give no reason other than general utility.

Turning to the feeling that accompanies the idea of justice, Mill thinks that it is derived from two basic sentiments that either are or resemble instincts: the impulse of self-defence, and the feeling of sympathy. But for these feelings to be justified, they must be subordinated to what is conformable to the common good. The strength of these feelings towards the protection of rights is different from the strength of the usual feeling towards general welfare, but this strength is justified on utilitarian grounds because it has to do with an extraordinarily important and impressive kind of utility: that of security. No human being can possibly do without security.

We depend on it for the value of every good beyond the passing moment. In summary, justice is the appropriate name for certain social utilities that are vastly more important, and therefore more absolute and imperative, than any others are as a class, and that therefore ought to be, as well as naturally are, guarded by a sentiment distinguished from the milder feeling that attaches to the mere idea of promoting happiness.

Thus, Mill feels that he has answered the objection that justice is distinct from utility. The modes of conduct required by justice can be given a utilitarian justification and, in cases of conflict between competing theories of justice, even require a utilitarian arbitration. And although the sentiment attached to instances of justice and injustice is different from that which attaches to utility in general, the very existence of that distinct and stronger sentiment has a utilitarian support.

V, 1–3

Mill states the problem of the chapter. The sentiment and idea of justice seem to be distinct from that of utility or happiness and sometimes to be in conflict with it. It has seemed to be an inherent quality in actions or states of affairs that they are just or unjust, rather than being derived from their utility. The feeling of justice might be a peculiar instinct, bestowed on us by Nature, but even so it might require, like other instincts, to be controlled and enlightened by reason. Even if instinctive, it is not infallible and may lead to wrong actions. But people are disposed to believe that any subjective feeling, not otherwise accounted for, reveals some objective reality; so it is necessary to attempt to ascertain the character of justice or of injustice. What is the quality, if there is any quality, attributed to all modes of conduct designated as just or unjust? If we can find such a quality, we can determine why it is capable of gathering around it a sentiment of that peculiar character and intensity.

The word 'sentiment' is not strong enough in the twenty-first century to convey the idea that Mill is concerned with. When people feel that an injustice has been done, whether to themselves or to a third party, they feel moral outrage. They feel indignation, anger, sometimes even hatred at the perpetrator. It is this feeling that Mill calls a 'sentiment of that peculiar character and intensity ...' (241 [V, 8]).

V, 4–10

In an effort to find the common character of all things just and unjust, Mill examines a list of six things that are known to excite the sentiments associated with those terms.

V, 5

In the first place, it is considered unjust to violate the *legal rights* of anyone. If a person is deprived of legitimate property, liberty, or life, we feel that an injustice has been done. But there are some exceptions. A person may have forfeited those rights. Mill does not here give examples, but some come to mind: that is, the usual explanations of how a person may be fined – losing some property rights; or imprisoned – losing some personal liberty; or executed – losing one's right to life. Mill, incidentally, spoke in Parliament to retain the death penalty. This may seem surprising, given his liberal political views, but he viewed the death penalty as being a more humane punishment than life imprisonment, also carrying a greater deterrent force. Criminals, he thought, would fear being hanged more than they would fear being imprisoned for life but in fact, he thought, being imprisoned for life would inflict more suffering.

V, 6

Secondly, it is considered unjust to deprive someone of that to which he has a *moral right*. Some legal rights are rights which are conferred by bad laws. Mill here raises the question of civil disobedience. If a law is a bad law, can it be disobeyed? Or should it be opposed only by attempting to get the law changed by legislative authority? Mill points out that those who oppose disobedience do so on grounds of expediency (utility), on the ground of the importance, to the common interest of mankind, of maintaining submission to the law. Mill makes an important distinction in this paragraph between bad laws – such that a different law or no law in its place would be better – and unjust laws, laws that violate rights that people ought to have recognized and respected. Some people hold that any bad law may be disobeyed, even if not judged to be unjust but only inexpedient; while others limit justified disobedience to the case of unjust laws. Some blur the distinction by saying that all bad laws are unjust, restricting liberty without tending towards any good. Common to all these differences of opinion, Mill says, there is agreement that a law can be unjust, in the same way that a breach of law is unjust, by infringing somebody's right. As it cannot be a legal right that is infringed, it is called a moral right.

Although Mill does not debate the merits of civil disobedience here but only points out the controversy, it is an important substantive issue. Is disobedience of unjust laws justified or even morally required? In Mill's lifetime there continued to be slavery in the USA. Were those who were assisting fugitive slaves doing what was morally right or even morally obligatory, although illegal? In more recent history, Gandhi in India and Martin Luther King, Jr. in the USA advocated non-violent disobedience to unjust systems of colonialism and segregation. What about violent or non-civil opposition to unjust institutions? Can they be justified?

What about a war considered unjust? Is resistance to conscription, not on the basis of total conscientious objection to all war but conviction that a particular war is unjust, justified? What about desertion by a military volunteer who joined out of trust that his or her country would engage only in wars of defence and not aggression, who has come to believe that an existing engagement is unjustified aggression? These are difficult questions. Is there a utilitarian answer or procedure for answering them? There is also the question of when a war is unjust. There is a tradition of 'just war' theory that rules when it is just to go to war and when a war is carried out in a just manner. For it to be just to go to war, there must be substantial aggression; non-belligerent correctives must either be hopeless or too costly; and belligerent correctives must be neither hopeless nor too costly. For a war to be conducted justly, harm to innocents should not be directly intended as an end or a means; and the harm resulting from the belligerent means should not be disproportionate to the particular defensive objective to be attained. These rules could be given utilitarian support, for they involve calculation of good and bad consequences, but are they sufficient? What about a preemptive war to prevent aggression? And if there is aggression, is only the victim group justified in defending itself, or can a third party intervene on humanitarian grounds? Can a war justly demand unconditional surrender from the aggressor, or is only a repulsion of the aggression justified? How can a distinction be made between innocent and non-innocent members of the enemy? And what counts as disproportionate harm? The application of utilitarian theory requires factual assumptions, and in particular cases there will be different opinions about the facts. Has substantial aggression occurred? Are non-violent responses hopeless? Will a response be too costly? Some utilitarians generalize that all wars are too costly, advocating pacificism or only non-violent resistance. Mill himself was not a pacifist, nor was he opposed in theory to military attempts to solve world problems. But he was sensitive to their limitations.

V, 7

Thirdly, it is considered just that each person get what he or she *deserves*, and unjust to obtain what he or she does not deserve. Mill is speaking here of common opinion concerning the *concept* of justice, in saying that a person is thought to deserve good from those to whom he or she has done good, and evil from those to whom he or she has done evil. 'The precept of returning good for evil has never been regarded as a case of the fulfillment of justice, but as one in which the claims of justice are waived, in obedience to other considerations' (242 [V, 7]). This principle of desert is the usual ground of 'retributive' punishment – making the criminal pay for what he has done. In general, the utilitarian tradition rejected this justification for punishment. Bentham asserted that any punishment is an evil, believing that the evil of punishment required justification by the good that came of it by means of deterrence, reform, or protection of society from the criminal. This tradition is in opposition to other theories of punishment demanding that a criminal suffer because he deserves to suffer, even if no future good comes of it. In the commentary on the preceding paragraph, we saw that Mill supported capital punishment. But he did so not on the grounds that a murderer deserves to die, or that the murderer should suffer the harshest penalty, but that the death penalty would have a deterrent effect upon other potential murderers and that the criminal would suffer *less* in dying than in being imprisoned for life.

V, 8

Fourthly, Mill says that it is regarded as unjust to *break faith* with anyone. Mill does not say so, but this obviously admits of degrees. There are promises and contracts that create expectations that are more or less serious. We do not apply the terms justice and injustice unless they are serious. But when we let people down who have depended upon us in serious ways, it is appropriate to say that this is unjust, quite apart from any legal obligations. Mill points out that like other obligations of justice, this is not absolute. There may be conflicting obligations of justice that override it, or the party may have forfeited the right to our keeping faith. There may also be promises that should not have been made. In that case it may be more unjust to keep the promise than to break it.

V, 9

Fifthly, justice requires *impartiality* in matters to which favour or preference do not properly apply. Mill points out that this requirement does not mean that one cannot give preference to caring for one's family or friends rather than strangers, and he says that impartiality where rights are concerned is involved in the notion of respect for rights. He also says that there are cases where impartiality means being influenced by desert, as in the administration of rewards and punishments. Where the public interest is concerned, impartiality requires being solely influenced by the public interest rather than the private. Mill summarizes this by saying that impartiality means being exclusively influenced by the considerations that ought to influence the particular case at hand and resisting any motives that would lead one to do otherwise. Does this analysis capture the notion of impartiality as a requirement of justice? Maybe Mill is too lenient on the preference that one can give to family and friends: 'A person would be more likely to be blamed than applauded for giving his family or friends no superiority in good offices over strangers, when he could do so without violating any other duty ...' (243 [V, 9]). Isn't this the kind of partiality that is considered unjust, where family or personal connection secures someone favourable treatment? Of course, it depends on circumstances. In a family business, to promote the prospects of one's child is not considered unjust. But if one is in a position to appoint someone to a public office, isn't appointing a member of one's family or a personal friend the kind of favouritism, bearing the derogatory name of nepotism? There is also the partiality of promoting the interest of people like oneself, of one's race, religion, gender, class, country of origin and so on. These are breaches of the justice of impartiality to which Mill seems to be insensitive. It is sensitivity to this kind of impartiality that programmes of equal employment opportunity and affirmative action are designed to engender.

V, 10

The idea of *equality* is part of the conception of justice and is considered by some to be its essence, but Mill says that there is great variety in conceptions of equality. It seems to vary with notions of utility. 'Each person maintains that equality is the dictate of justice, except where he thinks that expediency requires inequality. The justice of giving equal protection to the rights of all, is maintained by those who support the most outrageous inequality in the rights themselves' (243 [V, 10]). Slave societies, Mill says, do not regard slavery as unjust, because they think that slavery is expedient. 'Those who think that utility requires distinctions of rank, do not consider it unjust that riches and social privileges should be unequally dispensed ... Whoever thinks that government is necessary, sees no injustice in as much inequality as is constituted by giving to the magistrate powers not granted to other people' (244 [V, 10]).

Mill gives examples here of the diversity of 'the sense of natural justice' (ibid.). Should the produce of the community be shared on the principle of exact equality? Or is it just that those should receive more whose needs are greatest? Or should those receive more who work harder, or produce more, or whose services are more valuable to the community? These are alternatives that Mill does not explore in detail here, but they are important questions in analysing our 'sense of natural justice'. There is a difference between equality of *condition* and equality of *opportunity*. Equality of condition is a much more radical notion than equality of opportunity. If some people have more intelligence or talent than others, equality of opportunity may give them an advantage that equality of condition would attempt to redress. Is it just that people who have natural assets, such as good looks or good genes, should have advantages? Some inequalities in today's society could be overcome by Mill's proposals for universal education and freedom of choice to limit the number of children in a family. But what about inherited wealth and inherited 'human capital'? If someone is the child of a rich and educated family, won't that person have advantages that the child of a poor and uneducated family will lack? Can public schools be made as good as private money can buy in a private school? Can public educational institutions overcome the advantages of growing up in a family that is highly educated? What about cultural differences? Won't the child of a family that values education and hard work have incentives that another child will lack? What if a family's culture values having as many children as possible, even to the point of poverty?

On the other hand, there are natural and accidental disadvantages. Should there be special arrangements for those who are physically or mentally or emotionally handicapped? Are special parking places and ramps at taxpayers' expense an appropriate accommodation for the physically handicapped? What about higher teacher-student ratios for special education for the mentally handicapped? It is impossible to achieve equality of condition for the handicapped, but there are ways of attempting to come as close as possible. Are these requirements of justice?

Still another dimension to the discussion of equality is whether justice can be determined by patterns of distribution or only by the history of how the distribution took place. If someone wins a fair lottery, is that person's wealth therefore just, or does the inequality of wealth, in comparison with others, make it inherently unjust? Some people think that inheritance is like that. If you are intelligent, talented, good looking, energetic and have educated parents you are just lucky, and there is no injustice in the advantages that these bring. Others think that advantages derived from such natural luck are unfair and that there should be efforts to even the playing field by having public institutions give special help to the less advantaged. What about race or gender? If there is racial or gender discrimination in society, is 'affirmative action' to counter it morally required, or is it reverse discrimination and, therefore, unjust? In this paragraph Mill is pointing out the variations in our 'sense of natural justice'. He attributes them to variations in our beliefs concerning utility, but they seem to be more deep-rooted than that. We do seem to have a sense of natural justice that is distinct from utility, don't we? If we think that discrimination on the basis of race or gender is unjust, we don't simply think that such discrimination doesn't have the best consequences. In case there are differences of opinion about the justice of a policy, however, the way to approach these differences by rational argument may be only through an appeal to utility, especially an impartial assessment of utility. The question, 'How would you like it if you were the victim?' is such an appeal.

V, 11–12

Mill examines the etymology of the term 'justice' as a way of focusing on the essence of the concept. He says that in most if not all languages the etymology points to an origin connected with positive law – that is, law that has been enacted by a legislative authority – or authoritative custom, which is a primitive form of law. Reviewing the term for justice in Latin, Greek, German and French, he concludes that the primitive element in the formation of the notion of justice was conformity to law. Among nations that recognized that their laws were made by men, not directly by God, it was recognized that men could make bad laws, and these would permit actions that would be unjust if the law did not permit them. 'And hence the sentiment of injustice came to be attached, not to all violations of law, but only to violations of such laws as *ought* to exist, including such as ought to exist but do not; and to laws themselves, if supposed to be contrary to what ought to be law' (245 [V, 12]).

V, 13

Mill says that people do not limit the notion of justice to what is or ought to be regulated by law. 'Nobody desires that laws should interfere with the whole detail of private life; yet every one allows that in all daily conduct a person may and does show himself to be either just or unjust' (245 [V, 13]). But Mill says that even here the idea of law with its system of punishment lingers. 'When we think that a person is bound in justice to do a thing, it is an ordinary form of language to say, that he ought to be compelled to do it' (ibid.).

V, 14

Mill says that the idea of penal sanction, which is the essence of law, enters not only into the conception of justice but into that of any kind of wrong.

> We do not call anything wrong, unless we mean to imply that a person ought to be punished in some way or other for doing it; if not by law, by the opinion of his fellow creatures; if not by opinion, by the reproaches of his own conscience. This seems to be the real turning point of the distinction between morality and simple expediency. It is part of the notion of Duty in every one of

its forms, that a person may rightfully be compelled to fulfil it. (246 [V, 14])

There are other things that we wish people to do, that we like or admire them for doing, perhaps dislike or despise them for not doing, but we do not regard them as cases of moral obligation; we do not think that they are the proper objects of punishment. Mill says that there is no doubt that this is the distinction between what is right or wrong on the one hand, and what is merely desirable or praiseworthy on the other.

In this paragraph we see the strongest textual evidence that Mill is basically a rule-utilitarian. If punishment is the criterion of morality, morality is most conveniently thought of as a set of rules that are respected or violated, with punishment for their violation. However, someone interpreting Mill as an act-utilitarian might have two responses. First, the act-utilitarian might say that it is only one's conscience that punishes one for not doing the individual act that has the best consequences. Legal and social punishments enforce minimum moral standards embodied in public rules but utilitarian morality goes beyond that, requiring individuals to bear responsibility for unique cases. Punishment by one's own conscience is the penalty for not doing the best that one can. Second, it might be argued, having a set of moral rules enforced by sanctions is the most useful way for society to bring about the greatest conformity to the act-utilitarian principle. Act-utilitarianism is then the criterion of morally right acts, but enforcement of rules is the best strategy or 'decision procedure' for maximizing morally right acts. This is a plausible interpretation of Mill, common among commentators. On the other hand, as indicated in the reading of chapter 2, Mill seems to regard *morality* as primarily a matter of rules and precepts, with the ultimate principle of utility necessary only in cases of conflict and to guide the individual in exceptional cases, not a criterion to be applied to all individual acts. Morality is distinguished from the other branches of the 'Art of Life' by the sanctions that it condones, and in these other branches there may be more occasions for choice apart from rules. Morality is the enforcement of rules that are minimum standards. Punishment is the characteristic difference that marks off morality in general 'from the remaining provinces of Expediency and Worthiness; ...' (247 [V, 15]). There are acts going beyond morality that we admire or despise. There are lifestyles that we admire, and there are lifestyles that we disapprove of. The ones that we admire may be morally meritorious, praiseworthy. But failure to live up to those standards is not cause for moral blame. Some people, like saints and heroes, go beyond the call of duty. There are also lifestyles that we disapprove of, but we do not call them immoral unless we want to see such people punished. There may be great disagreement upon where to draw the line. Mill, in *On Liberty*, wants society not to interfere with mature individuals whose behaviour affects only themselves. If such people are lazy, or have addictions, or are not taking care of their health but are otherwise not failing to fulfil duties and are not harming other individuals, Mill wants them to have the liberty to live that way. They may not be contributing as much to the general welfare as they could, but Mill says that society can survive without their contributions and should do so to preserve individual liberty, arguing that individual liberty in general has great utility. Others, of course, would disagree with Mill and would want to enact paternalistic legislation to prohibit self-destructive behaviour, or they would at least want social opinion to penalize such people, not just attempt to persuade them to change their ways. But if people think that such behaviour should be controlled by penalties, Mill would say that they regard it as immoral, not just undesirable.

V, 15

Having identified what is morally wrong as that for which punishment is appropriate, Mill then marks off justice from other branches of morality. He refers to the distinction between perfect and imperfect duties. He says that imperfect duties are those that are obligatory, but the occasions of performing them are left to our choice. This is the nature of the duty of charity. One is obliged to be charitable, but no individual person has a right to our charity. Duties of perfect obligation are those in virtue of which a correlative *right* is attributed to some person or persons to whom the duty is owed. Mill reviews his survey of the characteristics of the concept of justice and injustice and finds that all of them involve respect for or violation of someone's right. If a person is treated better than he deserves, then this is a violation of the rights of competitors, who are assignable persons. So he concludes that this feature – a right in some person or persons correlative to the moral obligation –

constitutes the difference between obligations of justice and other moral obligations. Mill says that if one thinks that an assignable person has a right to our charity, then that duty is made one of justice: it is unjust not to fulfil our duty to that person. The distinction between perfect and imperfect duties was traditionally to distinguish between those duties that could be completely fulfilled, and those that are open-ended. Duties not to kill, steal, break a promise, etc., are all negative; it is possible completely to fulfil them. Duties to help others in distress are never completely fulfilled, because there are always people who are in distress and can be helped. So the distinction is traditionally between negative and positive duties. Does this correspond to Mill's distinction between duties that have a correlative right that can be claimed from one? It would seem that rights are then prohibitions: to have a right to life is to have a right not to be killed; to have a right to property is to have a right that it not be stolen or illegitimately taken away; to have a right to liberty is to have a right not to be interfered with in some respect. Can all rights be analysed as prohibitions against other people? Aren't some rights entitlements to positive behaviour on the part of other people and, if so, can they be completely fulfilled? A child may have a right to a parent's care, and there may be no limit to what that care entails. Is that a perfect obligation that can be completely fulfilled? There are also what are called 'welfare' rights: a right to a decent job, to decent housing, to healthcare and so on. In these cases, there are assignable people who are claimed to have the rights, but it is not clear what assignable people have the correlative duties to provide the services to meet the needs. Mill apparently does not have in mind these welfare rights, but he would have in mind the right of a child to proper care. Child neglect would be a case of injustice, but a parent's obligation to care for a child is open-ended; it would be an imperfect not a perfect obligation. Thus, Mill's identification of the perfect/imperfect distinction between obligations does not seem to correspond exactly with the distinction between duties of beneficence and those of justice. However, this does not affect Mill's main point, which is to claim that obligations of justice have a correlative right. 'Justice implies something which it is not only right to do, and wrong not to do, but which some individual person can claim from us as his moral right' (247 [V, 15]). Welfare rights could be accommodated to this description by saying that *society* has the obligation: there is something which it is not only right for society to do, and wrong not to do, but which some individual person who can claim from society as his moral right.

V, 16–21

Having analysed the *idea* of justice, Mill turns to the *sentiment* attached to that idea. He admits that the sentiment itself does not arise from anything that would commonly be termed an idea of expediency; but 'though the sentiment does not, whatever is moral in it does' (248 [V, 17]). He says that the sentiment has two essential ingredients, 'the desire to punish a person who has done harm, and the knowledge or belief that there is some definite individual or individuals to whom harm has been done' (248 [V, 18]). He claims that this desire to punish a person who has done harm to some individual is a spontaneous outgrowth of two natural feelings 'which either are or resemble instincts; the impulse of self-defence, and the feeling of sympathy' (248 [V, 19]). It is natural, he says, to desire to retaliate against any harm done to ourselves or to those with whom we sympathize. This is common throughout the animal kingdom. Every animal tries to protect itself and its young by attempting to retaliate against those who hurt or threaten it. Mill says that humans differ in only two ways. First, humans are capable of sympathy not just with their offspring or common herd but with all human or even all sentient beings. Second, humans are capable of conceiving of a community of interest between oneself and one's society so that anything that threatens the security of society generally calls forth the instinct of self-defence and urges resistance. This sentiment of self-defence, Mill says, 'in itself, has nothing moral in it; what is moral is, the exclusive subordination of it to the social sympathies, so as to wait on and obey their call. For the natural feeling tends to make us resent indiscriminately whatever any one does that is disagreeable to us; but when moralized by the social feeling, it only acts in the directions conformable to the general good: just persons resenting a hurt to society, though not otherwise a hurt to themselves' (249 [V, 21]). Is Mill correct here? Is the feeling that injustice has been done, and that the perpetrator deserves to suffer, limited to those acts that are contrary to one's conception of the general good? Mill attempts to answer this question in the next paragraph.

V, 22

Mill recognizes that it is common enough to feel resentment merely because we have suffered pain, but he asserts that if a person is regarding the act solely as it affects him individually, he is not paying attention to the justice of his actions. Mill says, 'a person whose resentment is really a moral feeling, that is, who considers whether an act is blameable before he allows himself to resent it – such a person, though he may not say expressly to himself that he is standing up for the interest of society, certainly does feel that he is asserting a rule which is for the benefit of others as well as his own' (249 [V, 22]).

Mill seems to be weakening his position here in saying that what is moral in the sentiment of justice is not necessarily the general good, but a rule for the benefit of others. How general must the benefit to others be, if it is not for the general welfare of society? If I am rich and resent having to pay graduated estate taxes, calling them unjust, I may recognize that estate taxes are for the benefit of society, but I claim that I deserve to bestow my wealth as I choose.

Mill says that if one is regarding an act solely as it affects oneself individually, one is not concerning oneself with the justice of one's actions. He claims that this is recognized even by anti-utilitarian moralists, and interprets Kant's fundamental principle of morals, 'So act, that thy rule of conduct might be adopted as a law by all rational beings', as virtually acknowledging that the interest of mankind must be in the mind of the agent when conscientiously deciding on the morality of the act. Mill tacitly recognizes that this is not the form that Kant's argument takes. Kant interprets his principle to be a law of reason, ruling out motives and intentions that cannot be universalized without contradiction. Mill thinks that this is to use

> words without meaning: for, that a rule even of utter selfishness could not *possibly* be adopted by all rational beings – that there is any insuperable obstacle in the nature of things to its adoption – cannot be even plausibly maintained. To give any meaning to Kant's principle, the sense put upon it must be, that we ought to shape our conduct by a rule which all rational beings might adopt *with benefit to their collective interest*. (ibid.)

Is Mill correct that the only plausible meaning of Kant's principle requires that the *collective interest* of rational beings must be included to give meaning to the principle? Here one might distinguish the *meaning* of Kant's principle from the *applications* or implications of Kant's principle. Kant intends to derive a rejection of utter selfishness from the principle on the grounds that it could not be willed without contradiction. Mill replies that there is no *inconceivability* in universal selfishness; there is nothing contradictory in willing universal selfishness; it is only that the *consequences* 'would be such as no one would choose to incur' (207 [I, 4]). So it may be that Mill is correct that Kant has failed to derive his rejection of utter selfishness without implicitly appealing to consequences. But there is some meaning left to Kant's principle. When Mill argues against lying on an occasion when the individual lie would have good consequences but amounts to the breaking of a rule of transcendent expediency, he says, 'If one person may break through the rule on his own judgment, the same liberty cannot be refused to others' (Mill 1852: 182). This seems to be an application of Kant's principle. A moral rule requires that it be general, that one cannot make an exception of oneself. From this it does not follow what rules need to be moral rules; that, according to Mill, would require a calculation of consequences, but it does say something meaningful about the structure of moral rules that is embodied in Kant's principle. Utter selfishness would be ruled out on the basis of consequences, not on the ground of inability to universalize it without contradiction, but the very structure of a moral rule requires some degree of universalizability.

V, 23

Mill summarizes his conclusion: justice includes two things; a rule of conduct and a sentiment that sanctions the rule. The first must be intended to be for the good of all mankind, with the conception of some definite person whose rights are violated by the infringement of the rule; the sentiment is a desire that punishment may be suffered by those who infringe the rule.

> And the sentiment of justice appears to me to be, the animal desire to repel or retaliate a hurt or damage to oneself, or to those with whom one sympathizes, widened so as to include all persons, by the human capacity; of enlarged sympathy, and the human conception of intelligent self-interest. From the latter

elements, the feeling derives its morality; from the former, its peculiar impressiveness, and energy of self-assertion. (250 [V, 23])

Notice that Mill has concluded that the rule of conduct must be *for the good of all mankind.* In his analysis of the idea of justice he has found the utilitarian criterion of morality. Is this a sound analysis? Can't there be an idea of justice as a rule of conduct to respect people's rights and for them to get what they deserve where the rights are protections for individuals or groups but not necessarily for the good of all mankind? There is the idea of justice in the protection of property rights, which benefit those who own property but do not necessarily benefit all mankind. There is the idea of justice in nations defending their borders against undocumented immigrants. Such an idea may be an appeal to national interest, not the good of all mankind. These seem to be counter-examples to Mill's concluding analysis of the idea of justice. Are they?

V, 24–5
Mill now gives a brief analysis of the idea of *right*, an idea that he has used in analysing the concept of justice. To have a right, he says, is 'to have something which society ought to defend me in the possession of' (250 [V, 25]). If someone asks why society ought, Mill says: 'I can give him no other reason than general utility' (250 [V, 25]). This is no surprise. Mill is now giving his own support for a theory of rights. But it ignores the alternatives to utilitarianism, such as a theory of natural rights, a theory of divine command, a theory of a social contract, or a theory of a natural sense. Elsewhere, we have discussed Mill's arguments against these theories, but if his arguments against them are inadequate, he must defend his own view as the best among the alternatives.

Mill attempts to deal with the objection that general utility does not seem to convey the strength of the obligation of justice nor the peculiar energy of the feeling. To this he replies that there goes into the feeling 'not a rational only but also an animal element, the thirst for retaliation; and this thirst derives its intensity, as well as its moral justification, from the extraordinarily important and impressive kind of utility which is concerned. The interest is that of security, to every one's feelings the most vital of all interests' (250–1 [V, 25]). Mill is pointing out not only that there is an instinctive non-rational basis for the sentiment, but the utility that is concerned is not *general* expediency. It is a smaller set of concerns that are more important. Many things that we desire we can do without; some things are desired or needed by some people and not by others – but no one can do without security. On it we depend '... for the whole value of all and every good, beyond the passing moment; since nothing but the gratification of the instant could be of any worth to us, if we could be deprived of everything the next instant by whoever was momentarily stronger than ourselves' (251 [V, 25]).

This is a significant argument. Protection of life, liberty and legitimate material possessions are the most important things that 'society ought to defend me in the possession of' (250 [V, 25]), and these are utilities, in the utilitarians' sense of utilities, meaning necessities for, or ingredients of, happiness. Mill says that the claim we have on society 'in making safe for us the very groundwork of our existence' thus generates feelings so much more intense than those concerned with the more common cases of utility that a difference of degree 'becomes a difference in kind. The claim assumes that character of absoluteness, that apparent infinity, and incommensurability with all other considerations' (251 [V, 25]).

In grounding the strength of the obligations of justice upon security, Mill's argument is reminiscent of the social contract argument of Thomas Hobbes (1588–1679) in his work *Leviathan* (1651). Hobbes thinks that there is no justice or injustice apart from the laws made by a sovereign that establish justice and injustice. But without such a sovereign to establish laws and enforce them with the power to punish, life would be insecure. In a 'state of nature', without a power to keep people in awe, each person has no security but what his own strength and his own invention can furnish him. In such condition, Hobbes concludes, there is 'continual fear and danger of violent death, and the life of man, solitary, poor, nasty, brutish, and short' (Thomas Hobbes 1950: 104 [pt. I, XIII, 9]). Hobbes claims that in a state of nature everyone has a natural right to everything, including the bodies and possessions of others, but because of insecurity it is rational for everyone mutually to transfer this right to a sovereign who will establish laws, respect for which amounts to justice and violation of which amounts to injustice, with the power to enforce them. This transfer of rights is a social contract, and Hobbes claims that this is the basis for legitimate political authority. Most political authority, Hobbes believes, comes about not by an actual transfer of right but by conquest. However, because it would be rational to engage in such a social contract to have a political sovereign – as long as the sovereign does indeed protect citizens' rights to life and property – it is a legitimate government and should be obeyed. Mill, of course, does not have the low opinion of human nature that Hobbes presents, but he does see the need for security as the fundamental utility that needs to be protected by a system of rights.

V, 26–31

Mill now gives examples of controversies concerning justice that he will attempt to connect to controversies regarding consequences. He thinks these *controversies* are evidence against an intuitionist account of justice. If justice 'be totally independent of utility and be a standard *per se*, which the mind can recognise by simple introspection of itself; it is hard to understand why that internal oracle is so ambiguous, and why so many things appear either to be just or unjust, according to the light in which they are regarded' (251 [V, 26]).

The intuitionists claim that utility is an uncertain standard with different people interpreting it differently and that the dictates of justice are immutable and unmistakable. Mill says that one would suppose from this that on questions of justice there could be no controversy, but 'there is as much difference of opinion, and as fierce discussion, about what is just, as about what is useful to society' (251 [V, 27]). Different nations have different notions of justice; different people within the same nation have different notions; Mill asserts that even in the mind of one individual justice is not one rule but many, which do not coincide in their dictates.

V, 28–9

An example is the justice of punishment. Mill gives four views: that it is unjust to punish someone as an example to others; that it is just only for the good of the sufferer himself; that it is unjust to punish someone for his own good; and, finally, that all punishment is unjustified.

The first of these views, that it is unjust to punish someone as an example to others, is a rejection of deterrence as a justification for punishment. Deterrence is one of the standard theories of just punishment. It is the theory that the threat of punishment deters would-be criminals who are calculating whether crime pays or not. If fear of punishment is included in the calculation, some criminals will be deterred from crime. Deterrence is one justification appealed to by utilitarians. Bentham had penetrating discussions on the topic. If a criminal is unlikely to be apprehended, then the punishment must be severe in order to deter. If apprehension is almost certain, then threat of a less severe penalty can deter. Bentham concluded that some behaviour, such as drunkenness and fornication, could be exterminated only by punishment a thousand times the possible mischief of the offence and, therefore, should not be criminalized. Only education and moral sanction should be used to combat them. Opposition to the theory of deterrence could be identified with one version of Kant's Categorical Imperative. One formulation of Kant is that one should act in such a way that one treats people never simply as a means, but always at the same time as ends in themselves. If punishing an offender is only for the benefit of society in general, that could be interpreted as using the criminal solely as a means to the end of lowering the crime rate.

The second theory, that punishment is just only when intended for the good of the sufferer himself, can be related to two quite different theories. One interpretation of punishment for the good of the criminal is the theory of Kant and Hegel (1770–1831). They argue that for punishment to be just it must be addressed to the criminal to make the criminal see the evil that he has done by having the evil done to him. Kant and Hegel's view is a justification of 'an eye for an eye, a tooth for a tooth' – not as a deterrent but as retribution. A murderer is to be murdered; a thief is to have his property taken from him. Mill has some discussion of this in the next paragraph when he discusses variation in the proper apportionment of punishments to offences. That discussion reflects differences in the justification of punishment being discussed here.

The other theory that punishment should be for the good of the criminal has the goal of reforming the criminal. This is evidently what Mill had in mind, and is another justification supported by utilitarian considerations. There is no reason that the intention to reform criminals should exclude the intention to deter further crime, except that some methods of reform work against deterrence. The intention to reform a criminal can take two quite different guises. One type of reform consist in pains inflicted on the criminal in hope that the criminal will be deterred from further crime by fear of further punishment; but reform can also take the form of providing the criminal with education and skills to find legitimate employment and not be driven by economic necessity to a further life of crime. The latter can work against deterrence, when deterrence is fear of punishment on the part of other would-be criminals. If apprehension for a crime results in free education and job training, it is not something to fear. Another way in which punishment can be seen as being for the benefit of the criminal is the therapeutic theory of response to crime. In this case, crime is seen as an illness that needs to be treated, primarily by removing the causes of crime, but also by treating criminals with psychological counselling and other methods of behaviour modification. In this view the treatment of the criminal is not called punishment, and it fits the Owenite theory (named after the Victorian social reformer Robert Owen) that crime is due to environmental influences that have shaped the personality of the criminal.

The third theory that Mill presents – that coercive efforts to modify a person's behaviour are unjust – is in opposition to reform when it is intended to change the criminal by painful punishments, education or therapy, not to address the criminal as a rational being. Hegel and Kant would denounce this as failure to respect the rationality of the human being. Some utilitarians might argue against reform as paternalistic, but that depends upon the nature of the crime. Mill says that people may justly be punished to prevent evil to others based on 'the legitimate right of self-defence' (252 [V, 28]). But if the crime is one of idleness, drunkenness, drug use, or deviant sexual behaviour with consenting partners, a utilitarian argument could be made, as Mill does in *On Liberty*, that these should not be criminalized so long as the harm is only to the individual agent.

Robert Owen believed that all behaviour is due to heredity and environment. As Mill states his view, he 'affirms that it is unjust to punish at all; for the criminal did not make his own character; his education, and circumstances which surround him, have made him a criminal, and for these he is not responsible' (ibid.). Owen did not reject measures to modify socially undesirable behaviour, but he did not want to call it punishment. Owen was a factory owner, and in front of each factory operative was a cube with a colour on each side. The overseer would each day turn a colour to represent the operative's work for the previous day. If it was excellent, the colour was white; if it was atrocious, it would be black. Thus, although not called punishment, there was a judgement, but a judgement not intended to make the agent pay for past offences, but to modify his behaviour for the future.

Mill's reason for presenting these conflicting theories of punishment is to argue that the concept of justice itself cannot settle the conflicts. 'All these opinions are extremely plausible; and so long as the question is argued as one of justice simply, without going down to the principles which lie under justice and are the source of its authority, I am unable to see how any of these reasoners can be refuted' (252 [V, 28]). Mill says that every one of the theories builds upon rules of justice that are recognized. One appeals to the injustice of singling out an individual and making him a sacrifice, without his consent, for other people's benefit. Another relies on the acknowledged justice of self-defence; another, on the injustice of forcing one person to conform to another's notion of what constitutes his good. The Owenite invokes the principle that it is unjust to punish anyone for what he cannot help. Mill says that each is triumphant so long as it is not compelled to take into consideration the other appeals. Mill says that to avoid the last of these, men imagined what they called the freedom of the will, 'fancying that they could not justify punishing a man whose will is in a thoroughly hateful state, unless it be supposed to have come into that state through no influence of anterior circumstances' (ibid.).

Mill himself held a view very close to Owen's with regard to free will, but he comes to a different conclusion regarding the justification of punishment. Mill holds the view that all events, including human actions, have causal determinants, but punishment can be one of the determinants of an individual's action and therefore justified. He calls his view the doctrine of 'necessity', although he believes that the term has misleading connotations. He depicts his opponents, holding the 'traditional' doctrine of 'free will', as believing that actions based on free will are unmotivated, that an action of free will is one going contrary to one's strongest motivation. Mill says that when I think that I am conscious of free will, what I am conscious of is a belief that after choosing one course of action, I could have chosen another *if I had liked it better*. It is not that I could have chosen one course while I preferred the other, all things considered. I often elect to do one thing when I should have preferred another 'in itself', apart from its consequences or from the moral law that it violates, and this preference for the thing-in-itself, abstracted from its accompaniments, is often loosely described as preference for the thing. Mill uses the example of murder:

> I am told, that if I elect to murder, I am conscious that I could have elected to abstain: but am I conscious that I could have abstained if my aversion to the crime, and my dread of its consequences, had been weaker than the temptation? ... [W]hen we think of ourselves hypothetically as having acted otherwise than we did, we always suppose a difference in the antecedents: we picture ourselves as having known something that we did not know, or not known something that we did know; which is a difference in external inducements; or as having desired something, or disliked something, more or less that we did; which is a difference in internal inducements. (Mill 1865: 451)

Mill claims that it is on the traditional doctrine of free will that punishment would not be justified. 'Punishment proceeds on the assumption that the will is governed by motives. If punishment has no power of action on the will, it would be illegitimate, however natural might be the inclination to inflict it. Just so far as the will is supposed free, that is, capable of action *against* motives, punishment is disappointed of its object, and deprived of its justification' (ibid., 458).

Mill concludes the paragraph in *Utilitarianism* by mentioning a theory of social contract such that members of society have engaged to obey the laws and consented to be punished for any disobedience to them; thus they have willed their own punishment when it is inflicted. Mill regards this as a 'mere fiction' (253 [V, 28]). Mill may have had in mind Hobbes, or he may have had in mind Rousseau (1712–1778), the author of *On the Social Contract* (1762). Rousseau argued that through a social pact by which a man submits his will to the general will of all citizens, the citizen consents to all the laws, even to those which punish him when he dares to break any one of them. Rousseau's conception of sovereignty is different from that of Hobbes. For Hobbes the sovereign who makes laws thus defining justice and injustice is a monarch or legislative body. For Rousseau the sovereign is the people, which cannot alienate their sovereignty. Magistrates and members of an assembly are always merely delegates, and the people have the right to remove them at all times.

Mill does not think that anything is gained by a theory of a social contract. For Mill a just constitutional arrangement and the legitimacy of laws are matters of good or bad consequences. Mill wrote a book, *Considerations on Representative Government*, in which he argues in favour of representative government at the same time that he sees problems with it. He bases his argument on utility, not on a social contract.

Is Mill correct that these principles of justice are all plausible and necessarily in conflict? That some thinkers have held each of them does not make them all plausible. Is it true that it is unjust to punish anyone for the sake of example to others? I don't think that Mill believed that. He favoured deterrent punishment. Is it true that punishment is just, only when intended for the good of the sufferer himself? I don't think that Mill believed that either. Is the reverse true, that it is never just to punish anyone for his own good? I don't think that Mill believed that. Finally, we have seen that although Mill agreed with Owen that circumstances have made the criminal, Mill does not regard this as grounds to reject punishment. Mill is putting these conflicting theories forward to assert that they are only partial truths. They are considerations that have plausibility, but they are not definitive of justice. They help to persuade the reader that utility is more fundamental than justice. Principles of justice are not self-evident. They require a foundation, and Mill believes that utility is the foundation and the arbiter in case of conflict between principles of justice.

V, 29

Mill here surveys differences of opinion about the proper apportionment of punishments to offences. The old morality of an eye for an eye, a tooth for a tooth is natural, and Mill says that although it has been generally abandoned in Europe, he believes that there is 'a secret hankering after it; and when retribution accidentally falls on an offender in that precise shape, the general feeling of satisfaction evinced, bears witness how natural is the sentiment to which this repayment in kind is acceptable' (253 [V, 29]). Mill gives other standards. One is that punishment should be measured by the moral guilt of the criminal, having nothing to do with the amount necessary to act as a deterrent. Another is that all punishment is an evil and that it is unjust to inflict any amount beyond the least that will suffice to prevent the criminal from repeating, and others from imitating, his crime. Mill does not point it out, but these theories of appropriate degree of punishment have much to do with the theories that justify punishment in the first place. The retributive standard, making the criminal pay for his crime by having done to him what he has done to others or making the punishment proportionate to the moral guilt of the criminal, are those espoused by Kant and Hegel who assert that the purpose of punishment is not to deter others but to make the criminal see what he has done and to do it to him. This standard would be rejected by utilitarians and by those who think that crime is due to heredity and environment, for which the criminal is not responsible. Utilitarians are most likely to hold the last view, and that any amount of suffering beyond its usefulness in reforming or deterring the criminal is unjust.

In giving examples of these conflicting views, Mill is attempting to bolster his argument that justice is not a standard independent of utility that can be known by introspection. Has he made his case?

V, 30–31

As indicated earlier, discussions of justice have traditionally distinguished between penal and distributive justice. In these two paragraphs Mill turns to topics of distributive justice – the justice of income and wealth distribution and the justice of alternative methods of taxation.

V, 30

Mill gives alternative theories of just income distribution: in accordance with talent or skill – assuming that those with superior talent or skill contribute more – or can demand more in a competitive market economy, or in accordance with effort. There are two more that Mill could have included, mentioned in paragraph 10, where he discusses equality: distribution in accordance with exact equality or in accordance with need. Here Mill gives the arguments for superior remuneration in accordance with talent or skill – that society receives more from such a person and owes more in return – and for remuneration in accordance with effort – that whoever does the best he can deserves equally well, and ought not to receive an inferior portion through no fault of his own. He also points out that those with superior skill or talent 'have already advantages more than enough, in the admiration they excite, the personal influence they command, and the internal sources of satisfaction attending them, without adding to these a superior share of the world's goods; and that society is bound in justice rather to make compensation to the less favoured, for this unmerited inequality of advantages, than to aggravate it' (254 [V, 30]).

Mill claims that from the point of view of justice alone, the conflict between these two views cannot be reconciled. 'Social utility alone can decide the preference' (ibid.). He might have added the argument that exact equality or distribution in accordance with need have appeals to our intuitions of justice and also have utilitarian support.

V, 31

Here Mill presents conflicting justifications for methods of taxation. One is that taxation should be in proportion to ability to pay, or that it should be graduated, taking a higher percentage from those with more to spare. Against this is the claim that each should pay the same absolute sum, as members of a club pay the same for the same privileges. The latter is supported by the assertion that the same protection of law and government is afforded to all; so there is no injustice in making all pay the same price. It is also supported by the example of a dealer charging the same price for the same merchandise, not a price varying according to the customer's means. Mill says that this doctrine, as applied to taxation, finds no advocates because it works against 'feelings of humanity and perceptions of social expediency' (254 [V, 31]). Mill was not aware of uses of the 'poll tax' to disenfranchise poor people in the USA in the late nineteenth century, nor the advocacy of a 'flat tax' in the twentieth and twenty-first. These were proposed, not on grounds of justice, but as an agency of injustice in the case of the poll tax and, with regard to the flat tax, as a proposal on specious economic grounds by the rich to avoid paying graduated taxes.

Mill discusses the claim that it is appropriate for the rich to pay more than the poor on the grounds that the State does more for the rich, protecting more property. Mill says that in reality this is not true, 'for the rich would be far better able to protect themselves, in the absence of law or government, than the poor, and indeed would probably be successful in converting the poor into their slaves' (255 [V, 31]). Is Mill correct about that? Would the rich be able to hire protection agencies to preserve their property whereas the poor would not? Or would the poor loot the property of the rich, taking everything of value? Mill then gives a compromise between the two, a proposal that everyone pay an equal tax for the protection of their persons, and an unequal tax for the protection of their property. Again, he concludes that these alternatives theories of the justice of taxation cannot be resolved by an intuitive appeal to justice. 'From these confusions there is no other mode of extrication than the utilitarian' (ibid.).

An alternative to Mill's claim that principles of distributive justice can only be settled by an appeal to utility is the theory of justice given by John Rawls in *A Theory of Justice* (1971). Rawls presents an ideal social contract theory as an alternative to utilitarianism. For Rawls, the social contract is not something that has historically occurred or even something that could have historically occurred. It is a way of conceiving of arguments for principles of justice that result in fairness, because the imagined conditions are fair. His vision proposes that members of a society choose principles of justice without knowing their place in that society (rich or poor, in positions of authority or not, and so on) and without even knowing their distinctive personal values (whether religious or not, what their life plans are, whether liberal or conservative and so on). He assumes that they are rational and self-interested but without envy, and that they have as much relevant information as can be given by the state of current science. To enable their self-interest to operate, Rawls assumes that they have the motivation to pursue certain goods that one would want, whatever other values one might have. These are more rather than less liberty and opportunity, wealth and income, power and authority, and the bases of self-respect. Under such conditions, Rawls argues, the principle(s) of justice chosen would not be the utilitarian principle, but would be two more specific principles, the first requiring equality in basic rights and duties; the second, that social and economic inequalities – for example inequality of wealth or authority – result in compensating benefits for everyone, and in particular for the least advantaged members of society. Rawls believes that these principles would rule out institutions that justify hardships on some for the greater good in the aggregate.

Why would people in the situation that Rawls describes not adopt the principle of utility? Wouldn't the expected utility of each person's welfare – the probability that one would have a certain level of welfare – be maximized by the maximization of the general welfare? Rawls argues against that conclusion by saying that there are risks that one would not want to take. Rawls claims that even if the average expected utility would be highest with utilitarian principles of justice, there could be some who would suffer unacceptable hardships for the greater good of the aggregate. It is interesting to see if Mill's theory of rights based on utility would have that result. Mill says that utilitarianism requires that each person's happiness – supposed equal in degree – should be counted for exactly as much as another's. 'All persons are deemed to have a *right* to equality of treatment, except when some recognized social expediency requires the reverse. And hence all social inequalities which have ceased to be considered expedient, assume the character not of simple inexpediency, but of injustice' (258 [V, 36]).

Does this provide a base line that would be equivalent to the two principles that Rawls puts forward? Rawls's first principle requires equality of rights and duties, a position that Mill supports. Mill advocates equal rights, not giving any advantage to a particular class, race, religion or sex. Rawls's second principle justifies inequalities if they result in compensating benefits for everyone, especially the least advantaged. Utilitarians generally recognize the principle of diminishing marginal utility – that wealth and income satisfy fewer wants and needs the more wealth and income one has. Thus, as a principle of distributive justice, a utilitarian would give priority to getting people out of poverty and ignorance before adding to the wealth of the rich. Rawls, citing Mill, recognizes that commonsense precepts of justice, particularly those that concern the protection of liberties and rights or that express the claims of desert, are supported by utilitarian considerations. But, he argues, 'there is no reason in principle why the greater gains of some should not compensate for the lesser losses of others; or more importantly, why the violation of the liberty of a few might not be made right by the greater good shared by many' (Rawls 1971: 26).

There is no reason 'in principle', but if utilitarian calculations in the real world come out in agreement with Rawls, there is substantive agreement between the theories. Rawls says that utilitarianism adopts for society as a whole the principle of rational choice for one person: 'Utilitarianism does not take seriously the distinction between persons' (Rawls 1971: 27).

The aggregate utility that is the goal of utilitarianism is impartial, but the system of rights that constitutes Mill's theory of justice admits that people are self-interested. Rights are protections of the security of self-interested individuals against other self-interested individuals, and this requires protection against loss of one's life, liberty and possessions for the marginally greater welfare of others. It is not clear that Mill's theory of justice would differ in its applications from that of Rawls.

V, 32–36

Having given his arguments against an intuitive foundation for principles of justice, Mill gives his summation that the principles of justice are not just subordinate to utility, but are the most important utilitarian considerations.

> I account the justice which is grounded on utility to be the chief part, and incomparably the most sacred and binding part, of all morality. Justice is a name for certain classes of moral rules, which concern the essentials of human well-being more nearly, and are therefore of more absolute obligation, than any other rules for the guidance of life; and the notion which we have found to be of the essence of the idea of justice, that of a right residing in an individual, implies and testifies to this more binding obligation. (255 [V, 32])

Mill says that the moral rules that forbid people from hurting one another, including wrongful interference with each other's freedom, are more vital than any rules that simply point out the best mode of managing some aspect of human affairs. 'It is their observance which alone preserves peace among human beings: if obedience to them were not the rule, and disobedience the exception, every one would see in every one else a probable enemy, against whom he must be perpetually guarding himself' (255 [V, 33]). Here again, one is reminded of Thomas Hobbes, who says that in a 'state of nature', where there is no power to make and enforce laws, there is a war of everyone against everyone. Mill goes on to say that mere instruction and exhortation to beneficence is not enough. People have an interest in each other's beneficence from time to time, but they are always in need that others should not do them harm. And it is these that constitute the obligations of justice. The same motives that command the observance of justice enjoin the punishment of those who violate them. Mill also includes disappointments of

117

expectation, in breach of friendship or breach of promise. Thus Mill says 'giving to each what they deserve, that is, good for good as well as evil for evil, is not only included within the idea of Justice as we have defined it, but is a proper object of that intensity of sentiment, which places the Just, in human estimation, above the simply Expedient' (256 [V, 34]).

Mill reviews some judicial maxims to argue that they are instrumental in carrying into effect the principles of justice so far stated. He says that the maxim that a person is only responsible for what he has done voluntarily, that it is unjust to condemn any person unheard, and that the punishment ought to be proportioned to the offence, are intended to prevent punishment from being arbitrary and ineffective.

The maxim of equality, Mill says, can be regarded as a corollary from the principle of treating each according to his deserts. Society should treat all equally when no duty forbids it. 'This is the highest abstract standard of social and distributive justice; towards which all institutions, and the efforts of all virtuous citizens, should be made in the utmost possible degree to converge' (257 [V, 36]). Mill says that this rests upon the very meaning of the greatest happiness principle, that each person's happiness, supposed equal in degree, is counted for exactly as much as another's. And the equal claim to happiness 'involves an equal claim to all the means of happiness, except in so far as the inevitable conditions of human life, and the general interest, in which that of every individual is included, set limits to the maxim; and those limits ought to be strictly construed' (258 [V, 36]).

Mill claims that there have been inequalities that in the past were believed to be necessary for the good of society. But when these have come to be believed unnecessary and inexpedient, they have come to have the character 'not of simple inexpediency, but of injustice, and appear so tyrannical, that people are apt to wonder how they ever could have been tolerated' (ibid.). So, he says, it has been 'the distinctions of slaves and freemen, nobles and serfs, patricians and plebeians; and so it will be, and in part already is, with the aristocracies of colour, race, and sex' (259 [V, 36]). Is Mill overlooking the fact that these distinctions were seldom viewed as having expediency for all society, but only for a party in power? Those in power may have tried to justify their superior position on claims of the inferiority of the weaker party. Those owning slaves may have claimed that a slave economy was beneficial for the nation, but did they really count the suffering of the slaves? More likely they justified their position on the ground that there were laws allowing slavery, so they were breaking no laws. And they tried their best to keep those laws in place, not because they were good for the slaves but because it was in their self-interest as slave owners not to lose their human property. When an institution of inequality is in place, there are claims that those with the inferior status prefer that status. Aren't these rationalizations instead of genuine estimates of utility? Of the examples that Mill mentions, the one that comes closest to being plausible is that of gender relations. For example, it may be claimed that women regard it as useful that they limit their role in family life to being wives and mothers and be subordinate to their husbands; but it is often the dominant party that primarily voices this view.

Mill is claiming in this paragraph that changes in beliefs about the justice of inequality are due to changes in assessments of the utility of the inequalities. There may be some truth to this view. When an economy is largely pre-industrial, a division of labour along gender lines may be efficient; but with industrialization, women and children as well as men could do efficient work outside the home in factories. If women could work in factories, why could they not also hold professional positions traditionally held by males? The loss of women's contributions to science and commerce could be seen as a fetter upon the efficiency of society, and this could be the basis for the assessment that discrimination against women in education and employment was unjust. There is some plausibility to this explanation. But isn't discrimination more than inefficiency? In Mill's effort to subordinate justice to utility, hasn't he overlooked claims made in the name of justice itself, independent of utility? Mill might reply that justice is associated with rights, and the question of what rights are justifiable is whether the rights, if protected by society, would have good consequences. In making claims against discrimination, victims are claiming equality as a right. But whether the right ought to be protected is, according to Mill, a matter of calculating consequences. Is this an adequate answer? Suppose oppressing a minority is for the greater good of the whole citizenry. Is it therefore just?

V, 37–8

Mill summarizes his conclusion. 'It appears from what has been said, that justice is the name for certain moral requirements, which, regarded collectively, stand higher in the scale of social utility, and are therefore of more paramount obligation, than any others' (259 [V, 37]). But Mill wants to recognize that there may be particular cases in which a right, and therefore justice, may be violated. He gives the example of it being allowable to steal food or medicine to save a life, thus violating someone's property rights. He says that to save a life, it may be allowable to coerce the only available medical doctor to care for that person, thus violating the doctor's right to liberty. But Mill says that we usually say that what is just in the ordinary case – respect for property or liberty – is not what is just in this case. 'By this useful accommodation of language, the character of indefeasibility attributed to justice is kept up, and we are saved from the necessity of maintaining that there can be laudable injustice' (ibid.).

Mill says that it has always been evident that cases of justice are cases of the promotion of utility. What has distinguished justice is the peculiar sentiment that attaches to cases of justice and injustice. He repeats his analysis of this sentiment: the natural feeling of resentment, moralized by being made co-extensive with the demands of social good; (259 [V, 38]), and he believes that this brings it into the compass of utilitarian ethics.

> Justice remains the appropriate name for certain social utilities which are vastly more important, and therefore more absolute and imperative, than any others are as a class (though not more so than others may be in particular cases); and which, therefore, ought to be, as well as naturally are, guarded by a sentiment not only different in degree, but also in kind; distinguished from the milder feeling which attaches to the mere idea of promoting human pleasure or convenience, at once by the more definite nature of its commands, and by the sterner character of its sanctions. (Ibid.)

Critical discussion questions

Mill's goal in this chapter is to show that utilitarianism and the demands of justice are not in conflict. His procedure is first to survey the characteristics of our common notions of justice and injustice to see what is most essential. He lists six characteristics: that it is unjust to deprive someone of his or her legal rights; that it is unjust to deprive someone of his or her moral rights; that it is just that each person gets what he or she deserves; that it is unjust to break faith with anyone; that it is inconsistent with justice to be partial; and, finally, that justice is associated with equality. Has Mill left out anything in the commonsense notion of justice and injustice? Has he given these characteristics appropriate weight? After he examines the etymology of the words, he concludes that what is essential is that unjust acts should be punished. Is that the essential idea, or are some of the other characteristics equally or more important? For example, a state of inequality, such as a group of people in poverty or homeless, may be considered unjust without an assignable culprit who deserves to be punished for it. Or it may be considered unjust that someone flourishes who doesn't deserve to flourish, without our being able to find someone to punish for it. Perhaps Mill has focused on unjust *acts*, without giving adequate attention to unjust *states of affairs*. There are unjust laws and traditions, unjust political systems, unjust economic systems, unjust status systems and so on that do not point to agents who deserve punishment, unless one points to those in power who could but do not change the system – and they perhaps deserve to be replaced with more responsible agents rather than punished.

Having claimed that penal sanction separates all of morality from general expediency, Mill appeals to the distinction between those duties in which a correlative right resides in some person or person and those moral obligations that do not give birth to any right. The violation of a right does seem generally to involve the idea of a personal right. Whether the injustice consists in depriving persons of possessions, or in breaking faith with them, or treating them worse than they deserve, in each case the victim can claim that a right has been violated. This can be true even if there is no agent who is responsible. So hasn't Mill unduly limited the idea of justice and injustice to obligations for which there are responsible agents?

A very important part of Mill's argument is to distinguish the *sentiment* of justice and injustice from the *rule of action* required by justice. When Mill analyses this feeling, he says that it involves the desire to punish a person who has done harm and the belief that there is some definite individual or individuals to whom harm has been done. Again, isn't Mill unduly restricting the object of the feeling in assuming that there is a person who has done the harm? The feeling of resentment and of sympathy that he ascribes to the feeling can be directed at the unjust condition without there being an identifiable culprit that one wants to retaliate against. When one of those with whom one sympathizes has been harmed, the anger may be without a clear target. Can't one just cry out against the failure of society in general to protect one, or against the nature of things that allows it to happen?

Mill next says that the sentiment must be 'moralized' by social feeling, that it is not moral unless it is the kind of hurt that society has a common interest in repressing. Isn't Mill here slipping in his utilitarian point of view? The sentiment may be that one has not got what one deserved without necessarily feeling that society would be better off if one had. For example, a rich person may resent having to pay estate taxes, claiming that he deserves to distribute the money as she wishes, at the same time admitting that the taxes can be used for social purposes that contribute to the general welfare more than the purposes for which she wants to use the money.

Mill says that when we call anything a person's right, we mean that he has a valid claim on society to protect him in the possession of it. But when asked why society ought to recognize such rights, Mill says that he can give no other reason than general utility. Here other theories of rights would diverge from Mill. Intuitionists would claim that they just know by intuition what rights people ought to have. Social contract theorists could tell a story about how there is a social compact underlying the rights, which does not necessarily require identity with general utility. Mill does not recognize these alternatives; so the question is, has he provided a better account than the alternatives?

One of Mill's arguments against intuitionists is that there is great controversy about what policies in punishment, wages and taxation are just and unjust. If justice is something that the mind can recognize by simple introspection, it is hard to understand why there is so much controversy. But is this a refutation of intuitionism? People have grown up with different educations, and not all of them have led to true beliefs. Some of the divergent theories of what justice is may be false. I think Mill believes that the theory of 'an eye for an eye' is a false theory. An intuitionist who believes that the retributive theory is true would say that any other theory is false, due, perhaps to the corrupting influences of utilitarianism. Mill claims that the divergence in opinions is due to differences in estimates of utility, but is that true? Isn't it more likely to be assumptions about justice that are independent of utility, such as what one deserves?

Mill is correct that there can be a utilitarian basis for a system of rights to protect people in that most important concern, that of security. He is correct that utility can provide a basis for a utilitarian conception of justice and even for a 'moralized' special feeling in regard to justice and injustice. But there are alternative systems of rights, and there are alternative foundations for defending those rights. The persistent question is whether Mill's utilitarianism provides the best of the alternatives.

Study questions

Can the 'sentiment' of justice be distinguished from the 'rule of action' required by justice?
Is justice that set of moral obligations that are correlated with rights?
Has Mill proved that justice is subordinate to utility?

SUMMARY

Mill has attempted to answer the major objections to utilitarian ethics. In response to the objection that it is a doctrine only worthy of swine, he has introduced the notion of the qualitative superiority of pleasures that can be experienced only by human beings. The criterion of qualitative superiority is the preference of those who are acquainted with different pleasures and are good at self-observation and analysis of their preferences. Mill also attempts to answer other objections: that happiness is unattainable; that doing without happiness is a necessary condition for all virtue; that it is expecting too much for people to be always acting for the promotion of the general happiness; that utilitarianism is a godless doctrine; that utilitarianism allows agents to do what is expedient instead of acting on principle; that there is not time prior to action to calculate the act's effects on the general happiness; and that utilitarianism allows agents to make their own case an exception to moral rules. All of these are addressed in chapter 2, and they have been discussed above in 'Reading the Text'. Mill then, in chapter 3, discusses motivation for conforming to moral rules, and he argues that utilitarianism has all the sanctions that can be applied to any moral system but that in addition, as civilization progresses and people find their welfare tied up with the welfare of others, an additional motive is supplied for conformity with a utilitarian ethics. In chapter 4, Mill gives a psychological argument for happiness as inclusive of all things that are valued as ends; and in chapter 5, he attempts to show that justice in not in conflict with utility but is a most important concern for a utilitarian moralist.

This summarizes the aims of the work. It is for the perceptive reader to evaluate these arguments and to determine whether Mill has been successful.

CHAPTER 4

RECEPTION AND INFLUENCE

J. B. Schneewind, in 'Concerning some criticisms of Mill's *Utilitarianism*, 1861–76' (Schneewind 1976), made a study of the early reception of Mill's *Utilitarianism*. He says that at the time Mill's work was written, there was no readily available systematic exposition of the secular utilitarian point of view. Most of the earlier eighteenth and nineteenth century utilitarians held theological versions of utilitarianism. William Paley (1743–1805), who was best known among these, was conservative as well as religious. Bentham's *Introduction to the Principles of Morals and Legislation* was not reprinted separately between 1823 and 1876. The universities of Scotland were dominated by anti-utilitarians. Mill's *Logic* was taught at Oxford, but not utilitarian ethics.

When John Stuart Mill published *Utilitarianism*, he was the foremost philosopher of Britain. He was best known, however, for his *Logic*, his *Principles of Political Economy*, his essay *On Liberty* and his contributions to periodicals. *Utilitarianism*, first published in *Fraser's Magazine*, did not receive much critical attention, and what there was was critical. He was opposed not only by intuitionists, who were the target of the essay, but also by religious writers, who preached that utilitarianism was a corrupting philosophy. With the publication in 1869 of W. E. H. Lecky's *History of European Morals*, Mill began to receive more attention. Lecky had made a survey of the two great positions in Victorian ethics – the intuitional and the utilitiarian. Lecky was strongly opposed to utilitarianism, and his criticisms were answered by Mill's friend John Morley and by Fitzjames Stephen, who defended utilitarianism, although Stephen was a critic of Mill's *On Liberty*. Lecky fails to mention Mill, and those who agreed with Lecky in his opposition to utilitarianism felt that he had failed to come to grips with the best version of the theory, which was thought to be Mill's. The first book length study of *Utilitarianism* was *An Examination of the Utilitarian Philosophy* by John Grote, published in 1870. In 1872 Calderwood's *Handbook of Moral Philosophy* said that Mill's is now the accredited type of utilitarianism, and in 1874 T. R. Birks published his lectures *Modern Utilitarianism*, surveying Bentham and Paley as well as Mill, criticizing Mill's doctrine at length. Henry Sidgwick in 1874 published *Methods of Ethics*, an important volume in the history of ethics. Sidgwick was sympathetic to utilitarianism, but he had objections to two or three of Mill's central contentions. F. H. Bradley (1846–1924), a British Idealist philosopher and an important ethicist of the late nineteenth century, included an essay 'Pleasure for Pleasure's Sake' in *Ethical Studies* (1876). Mill is the central individual target of his attack on hedonism and utilitarianism.

J. B. Schneewind, in his study, says that almost all of the attention to Mill in the first fifteen years after *Utilitarianism* appeared was hostile. Schneewind analyses four main points: the derivability of moral notions from non-moral notions; the 'proof' of the principle of utility; the distinction between higher and lower pleasures; and the claim that the rules of commonsense morality may be taken as secondary principles of utilitarian ethics. Grote's book reflected most of the critical comment of other reviewers.

On the first point, it was argued that in the statement, 'Honesty is the best policy', the *idea* of honesty is one thing and the *idea* of policy is another. Lecky claims that all languages and all peoples distinguish between the ideas of interest and utility on the one hand and of virtue on the other. Grote develops this contrast as a contrast between the ideal and the actual, between what ought to be and what is. 'Right' does not mean 'conducive to happiness'. Others asserted that moral goodness is not complex and resolvable into simpler elements, but is itself a simple concept.

On the proof, early critics pointed out what they claimed to be a false analogy between 'visible' and 'desirable'. Another criticism was that the observation that each man desires his own happiness is no reason for saying that the general happiness is desirable. Another criticism was to reject the claim that equal amounts of happiness are equally desirable. To whom is A's happiness as desirable as an equal lot of B's? Grote says that observation cannot show that man desires the desirable if by the desirable is meant the *ideally desirable*. And even if each desires his own happiness, we can hardly conclude, he claims, that the happiness of the aggregate is a good to the aggregate, for the conclusion is meaningless unless the aggregate can have desires. Sidgwick claims that from the fact that each man desires his own happiness, the natural inference – if one were allowed – would be not universalistic hedonism, which is Mill's conclusion, but egoistic hedonism. But Sidgwick rejects Mill's psychology – that each man desires only his own happiness.

Most critics claimed that if there are different qualities of pleasure, an independent, non-hedonistic standard has been introduced. Grote objects to separating pleasures out as objects of comparison from the activities in the course of which they occur. Sidgwick holds that to be consistent, all qualitative comparison of pleasures must resolve itself into quantitative comparison. Only John Morley, in a review of Lecky, defends Mill's distinction.

Regarding the claim by Mill that commonsense morality is based on what we have learned are the consequences of various kinds of actions and can thus be viewed as utilitarian secondary principles, Sidgwick points out that they are not held as beliefs about the best ways of achieving general happiness. He claims that there is a categorical difference between actions that are immediately preferable and actions that are regarded as means to an end. Bradley also makes this criticism. The commonsense rules of morality bind us in a much stronger way than guides to general welfare. 'Do not commit adultery' is a law to be obeyed, not a prescription of a probable best policy. These early criticisms are the most common that have been voiced in the succeeding years. But more recent supporters of Mill have answered them. There are a significant number of Mill scholars who think that the criticisms can be answered, either because they are misunderstandings of Mill, or because they are fallacious arguments, or both. Much of the philosophical literature on Mill's essay in the twentieth century amounted to repetitions of the early criticisms and answers to them.

Before Mill wrote, according to Schneewind, utilitarianism was seen as subversive of morality and irreconcilable with the central doctrines of Christianity. It was blamed for political corruption, the decline of commercial good faith and the decay of female decorum. The pre-Millian utilitarians were so critical of accepted morality that intuitionists did not think that accepted morality was being taken seriously. Mill's higher/lower analysis of pleasures, and his treatment of accepted moral rules as wisdom of past experience, helped the intuitionists to treat utilitarianism as a serious philosophical theory. The result was philosophical criticism of utilitarianism's adequacy as a sound account of moral convictions. This was due to Mill. *Utilitarianism* was meant to remove popular antipathy and suspicion about the doctrine and also to convince the philosophical community of the soundness of the position. Mill's utilitarianism sought to incorporate the insights of previously opposed thinkers, and the response was that critics came to see utilitarianism as having an important contribution to make to moral philosophy in spite of its deficiencies. This is found in Sidgwick and even in Bradley. Bradley says that utilitarianism's heart is in the right place, but the brain is lacking. Thus Mill's essay, within fifteen years, achieved the aim of obtaining for utilitarianism an honoured place among philosophers.

In the late nineteenth century and early twentieth century, important philosophers adopted the consequentialist part of utilitarianism but rejected its hedonism. G. E. Moore (1873–1958), in *Principia Ethica* (Moore 1903), accepted a definition of the 'right' as meaning 'cause of a good result', thus accepting by definition a kind of act-consequentialism. But he attacked Mill as having committed the 'naturalistic fallacy' in defining 'good' as 'pleasure'. The 'naturalistic fallacy' was to define a 'non-naturalistic' word by a word of nature. Moore interpreted 'good' as a non-naturalistic word and 'pleasure' as descriptive of something in nature. This is a misreading of Mill, for Mill did not *define* good as pleasure, but it had the effect of calling attention to Mill's essay as the object of Moore's attack. Moore was one of the leading philosophers of Britain at the time, and his misreading of Mill led other philosophers to attempt to correct the mistake. Moore was an intuitionist regarding what is good. According to Moore, one has intuitions of what is good, and these include knowledge and beauty, not just pleasure. Hastings Rashdall (1858–1924) in *The Theory of Good and Evil* (Rashdall 1907) coined the term 'ideal utilitarian' to describe his position, and that could apply to Moore as well. Rashdall accepted the utilitarian view that actions are to be judged by their tendency to produce the greatest good or wellbeing for human beings, but he believed that this good is not confined to pleasure and prevention of pain. Among the goods are the moral value of the agent of the action. In doing a right act, an agent's virtue is part of the value of the act.

Moore's version of utilitarianism was an 'act-utilitarian' version, and that became the standard version for discussion in the twentieth century. That version was read into Mill's essay, in spite of contrary evidence, until challenged by J. O. Urmson in 1953 (Urmson 1953: 33–40). Whether Mill was an act-utilitarian or a rule-utilitarian became a more prominent dispute after rule-utilitarianism was defended, independently of the interpretation of Mill, by John Rawls (Rawls 1955: 3–32), by Richard Brandt (Brandt 1959), and others. Numerous articles and discussion in books dealt with that controversy, some seeing Mill as holding an act-utilitarian theory of right action but a 'strategic' rule-utilitarian theory of how most effectively to achieve the maximum number of right acts. As shown above in 'Reading the Text', Mill's theory is quite complex, including not only rules but rights, and limiting moral rules to allow for meritorious acts going beyond the call of duty.

In the course of the twentieth century, Mill's *Utilitarianism* became the standard work representing utilitarianism. It was assigned as required reading in many courses on ethics or moral philosophy, and it became a 'set text' for examinations in philosophy in many British universities. When taught and studied so widely, the details became subjects of great controversy. Mill's 'proof' in chapter 4 is an example. J. B. Schneewind, in his introduction to *Mill's Ethical Writings* (1965) could say, 'In the last fifteen years there have been more essays dealing with the topic of "Mill's Proof" than with any other single topic in the history of ethical thought' (Schneewind 1965: 31). In the years after 1965 the number increased even more.

The influence of Mill and of utilitarianism is seen not only by those who have studied Mill's text but also by those who see Mill or utilitarianism as the most important alternative to their theory. Examples are intuitionists, such as W. D. Ross in *The Right and the Good* (Ross 1930) and E. F. Carritt in *Ethical and Political Thinking* (Carritt 1947). John Rawls, in *A Theory of Justice* (Rawls 1971), his important effort to present an ideal social contract theory of justice, regards utilitarianism, although it is not exactly Mill's version, as the chief alternative to his approach.

In current textbooks, Mill is often contrasted with Kant as one of the two great moral thinkers of modern times. For example, one textbook, *Moral Philosophy: Classic Texts and Contemporary Problems* (Feinberg *et al.* 1977), in the section 'Three Classic Theories', contains selections from Aristotle's *Nicomachean Ethics*, selections from Kant's *Fundamental Principles of the Metaphysics of Morals* and the complete text of Mill's *Utilitarianism*.

In assessing the influence of Mill's *Utilitarianism*, it is difficult to separate the influence of Mill's essay from the influence of utilitarianism as a philosophy. Many philosophers call themselves consequentialists without endorsing Mill's hedonism or the detailed arguments in his work. Outside of philosophy, concern for consequences has been a prevailing motive in policy decisions. What are the (probable) costs, and what are the (probable) benefits, and do the expected benefits outweigh the expected costs? This mode of thinking cannot be attributed to the influence of Mill's essay, and it is usually carried out by a measurement of monetary costs and benefits rather than pleasures and pains. When there is an effort to get beyond monetary measures, the measures are usually efforts to measure existing preferences, rather than the preferences that people would have if they were fully informed and experienced in alternatives, which would be Mill's criterion. Nevertheless, we can say that Mill is a representative of utilitarianism, and utilitarian thinking has had a major impact on policy studies since his time.

In an educational video entitled 'Ethics in America', there is a picture of four names that are supposed to be representative of the great ethical thinkers in western philosophy. They are Plato, Aristotle, Kant and Mill. What more need we say of the recognition of Mill's importance?

NOTES FOR FURTHER READING

SECONDARY MATERIAL

Alican, Necip Fikri (1994), *Mill's Principle of Utility: A Defence of John Stuart Mill's Notorious Proof*. Amsterdam and Atlanta: Rodopi.

Anderson, Susan Leigh (2000), *On Mill*. Belmont, CA: Wadsworth.

Berger, Fred R. (1984), *Happiness, Justice, and Freedom: The Moral and Political Philosophy of John Stuart Mill*. Berkeley and Los Angeles: University of California Press.

Brown, D. G. (1973), 'What is Mill's principle of utility?' *Canadian Journal of Philosophy* 3, 1–12.

Cooper, Neil (1969), 'Mill's "proof" of the principle of utility'. *Mind* 78, 278–9.

Cooper, Wesley E., Kai Nielsen, and Steven C. Patten, (eds) (1979), *New Essays on John Stuart Mill and Utilitarianism. Canadian Journal of Philosophy*, supp. vol. 5. Guelph: Canadian Association for Publishing in Philosophy.

Copp, David (1979), 'The iterated-utilitarianism of J. S. Mill', in Wesley E. Cooper, Kai Nielsen, and Steven C. Patten (eds), *New Essays on John Stuart Mill and Utilitarianism. Canadian Journal of Philosophy*, supp. vol. 5. Guelph: Canadian Association for Publishing in Philosophy.

Crisp, Roger (1997), *Mill on Utilitarianism*. London and New York: Routledge.

Donner, Wendy (1991), *The Liberal Self: John Stuart Mill's Moral and Political Philosophy*. Ithaca: Cornell University Press.

——— (1998), 'Mill's utilitarianism', in John Skorupski (ed.), *The Cambridge Companion to Mill*. Cambridge: Cambridge University Press, pp. 255–92.

Edwards, Rem B. (1979), *Pleasures and Pains: A Theory of Qualitative Hedonism*. Ithaca: Cornell University Press.

Gruzalski, Bart (1981), 'Foreseeable consequence utilitarianism'. *Australasian Journal of Philosophy* 59, 163–76.

Gunderson, Martin (1998), 'A Millian analysis of rights'. *Ideas y Valores* 106, 3–17.

Hall, E. W. (1949–50), 'The "proof" of utility in Bentham and Mill'. *Ethics* 60, 1–18.

131

Harrod, R. F. (1936), 'Utilitarianism revised'. *Mind* 45, 137–56.

Kretzman, N. (1958), 'Desire as proof of desirability'. *Philosophical Quarterly* 8, 246–58.

Lyons, David (1976), 'Mill's theory of morality'. *Nous* 10, 101–20.

——(1978), 'Mill's theory of justice', in A. I. Goldman and J. Kim (eds), *Values and Morals: Essays in Honor of William Frankena, Charles Stevenson, and Richard Brandt*. Dordrecht: Reidel, pp. 1–20.

——(1982), 'Benevolence and justice in Mill', in Harlan B. Miller and William H. Willams (eds), *The Limits of Utilitarianism*. Minneapolis: University of Minnesota Press, pp. 42–70.

——(1994), *Rights, Welfare, and Mill's Moral Theory*. New York and Oxford: Oxford University Press.

——(ed.) (1997), *Mill's* Utilitarianism: *Critical Essays*. Lanham, MD: Rowman and Littlefield Publishers.

Mabbott, J. D. (1956), 'Interpretations of Mill's *Utilitarianism*'. *Philosophical Quarterly* 6, 115–20.

Mandelbaum, Maurice (1968), 'On interpreting Mill's *Utilitarianism*'. *Journal of the History of Philosophy* 6, 35–46.

——(1968), 'Two moot issues in Mill's *Utilitarianism*', in J. B. Schneewind (ed.), *Mill: A Collection of Critical Essays*. Garden City, NY: Doubleday.

Martin, Rex (1972), 'A defence of Mill's qualitative hedonism'. *Philosophy* 47, 140–51.

McCloskey, H. J. (1971), *John Stuart Mill: A Critical Study*. London and Basingstoke: Macmillan.

Miller, Dale (1998), 'Internal sanctions in Mill's moral psychology'. *Utilitas* 10, 68–82.

Miller, Harlan B., and William H. Willaims (eds) (1982), *The Limits of Utilitarianism*. Minneapolis: University of Minnesota Press.

Ryan, Alan (1974), *J. S. Mill*. London and Boston: Routledge and Kegan Paul.

——(1988), *The Philosophy of John Stuart Mill*, 2nd edn London: Macmillan.

——(ed.) (1968), *Mill: A Collection of Critical Essays*. Garden City, NY: Doubleday; London: Macmillan.

Seth, James (1908), 'The alleged fallacies in Mill's "Utilitarianism"'. *The Philosophical Review* 17, 469–88.

Shaw, William H. (1999), *Contemporary Ethics: Taking Account of Utilitarianism*. Malden, MA, and Oxford: Blackwell Publishers.

Skorupski, John (1989), *John Stuart Mill*. London and New York: Routledge.

——(ed.) (1998), *The Cambridge Companion to Mill*. Cambridge: Cambridge University Press.

Smart, J. J. C. (1956), 'Extreme and Restricted Utilitarianism'. *Philosophical Quarterly* 4, 344–54.

Sumner, L. W. (1974), 'Welfare, happiness, and pleasure'. *Utilitas* 4, 199–223.

West, Henry R. (1976), 'Mill's qualitative hedonism'. *Philosophy* 51, 101–5.

——(1982), 'Mill's "proof" of the principle of utiity', in Harlan B. Miller and William H. Williams (eds). Minneapolis: University of Minnesota Press.

——(2004), *An Introduction to Mill's Utilitarian Ethics*. Cambridge: Cambridge University Press.

——(ed.) (2006), *The Blackwell Guide to Mill's* Utilitarianism. Malden, MA, and Oxford: Blackwell Publishing.

SELECTIVE BIBLIOGRAPHY (WORKS REFERRED TO)

Aristotle (1941), *Nicomachean Ethics*, in Richard McKeon (ed.), *The Basic Works of Aristotle*. New York: Random House, pp. 935–1112.

Bentham, Jeremy (1970; first published 1789), *An Introduction to the Principles of Morals and Legislation*. London: University of London, Athlone Press.

Birks, Thomas Rawson (1874), *Modern Utilitarianism*. London.

Bradley, F. H. (1927; first published 1876), *Ethical Studies*, 2nd edn London: Oxford University Press.

Brandt, Richard (1959), *Ethical Theory*. Englewood Cliffs, NJ: Prentice-Hall.

Calderwood, Henry (1872), *Handbook of Moral Philosophy*. London.

Carritt, E. F. (1947), *Ethical and Political Thinking*. Oxford: Clarendon Press.

Feinberg, Joel, and Henry West (eds) (1977), *Moral Philosophy: Classic Texts and Contemporary Problems*. Encino, CA: Dickenson.

Grote, John (1870), *An Examination of the Utilitarian Philosophy*. Cambridge: Deighton, Bell, and Co.

Hobbes, Thomas (1950; first published 1651), *Leviathan*. New York: E. P. Dutton and Company.

Kant, Immanuel (1785), *Fundamental Principles of the Metaphysics of Morals*. Indianapolis: The Bobbs-Merrill Company, 1949.

Lecky, William Edward Hartpole (1869; 3rd edn, 1890), *History of European Morals*. 2 vols. New York: D. Appleton.

Mill, James (1869), *Analysis of the Phenomena of the Human Mind*, 2nd edn (1st edn, 1829). 2 vols. John Stuart Mill (ed.). Reprint, New York: Augustus M. Kelley, 1967.

Mill, John Stuart (1833), 'Remarks on Bentham's philosophy', in J. M. Robson (ed.), *Essays on Ethics, Religion and Society*. Vol. 10 of *Collected Works of John Stuart Mill*. Toronto: University of Toronto Press, 1969, pp. 3–18.

——(1835), 'Sedwick's discourse', in J. M. Robson (ed.), *Essays on Ethics, Religion and Society*. Vol. 10 of *Collected Works of John Stuart Mill*. Toronto: University of Toronto Press, 1969, pp. 31–74.

——(1838), 'Bentham', in J. M. Robson (ed.), *Essays on Ethics, Religion and Society*. Vol. 10 of *Collected Works of John Stuart Mill*. Toronto: University of Toronto Press, 1969, pp. 75–116.

——(1840), 'Coleridge', in J. M. Robson (ed.), *Essays on Ethics, Religion and Society*. Vol. 10 of *Collected Works of John Stuart Mill*. Toronto: University of Toronto Press, 1969, pp. 117–64.

——(1843; 8th edn, 1871), *A System of Logic: Ratiocinative and Inductive*. Vols. 7–8 of *Collected Works of John Stuart Mill*. Toronto: University of Toronto Press, 1974.

——(1848; 6th edn, 1871), *Principles of Political Economy*. Vols. 2–3 of *Collected Works of John Stuart Mill*. Toronto: University of Toronto Press, 1965.

——(1852), 'Whewell on moral philosophy', in J. M. Robson (ed.), *Essays on Ethics, Religion and Society*. Vol. 10 of *Collected Works of John Stuart Mill*. Toronto: Toronto University Press, 1969, pp. 165–202.

——(1859), *On Liberty*, in J. M. Robson (ed.), *Essays on Politics and Society*. Vol. 18–19 of *Collected Works of John Stuart Mill*. Toronto and Buffalo: University of Toronto Press, 1977, vol. 18, pp. 213–310.

——(1861), *Considerations on Representative Government*, in J. M. Robson (ed.), *Essays on Politics and Society*. Vol. 18–19 of *Collected Works of John Stuart Mill*, 1977, vol. 19, pp. 371–578.

——(1861a), *Utilitarianism*, in J. M. Robson (ed.), *Essays on Ethics, Religion and Society*. Vol. 10 of *Collected Works of John Stuart Mill*. Toronto: University of Toronto Press, 1969, pp. 203–60.

——(1865; 4th edn, 1872), *An Examination of Sir William Hamilton's Philosophy*. Vol. 9 of *Collected Works of John Stuart Mill*. Toronto and Buffalo: University of Toronto Press.

——(1865a), *Auguste Comte and Positivism*, in J. M. Robson (ed.), *Essays on Ethics, Religion and Society*. Vol 10 of *Collected Works of John Stuart Mill*. Toronto: University of Toronto Press, pp. 261–368.

——(1868), 'Letter to Henry Jones, June 13, 1868', in Francis E. Mineka and Dwight N. Lindley (eds), *The Later Letters of John Stuart Mill 1849–1874*. Vols. 14–17 of *Collected Works of John Stuart Mill*. Toronto and Buffalo: University of Toronto Press, 1972, vol. 16, p. 1414.

——(1869), *The Subjection of Women*, in J. M. Robson (ed.), *Essays on Equality, Law, and Education*. Vol. 21 of *Collected Works of John Stuart Mill*. Toronto and Buffalo: University of Toronto Press, pp. 259–340.

——(1873), *Autobiography*, in John M. Robson and Jack Stillinger (eds), *Autobiography and Literary Essays*. Vol. 1 of *Collected Works of John Stuart Mill*. Toronto and Buffalo: University of Toronto Press, 1981, pp.1–290.

——(1874), 'Nature', in *Three Essays on Religion*, in J. M. Robson (ed.), *Essays on Ethics, Religion and Society*. Vol. 10 of *Collected Works of John Stuart Mill*. Toronto: University of Toronto Press, 1969, pp. 373–402.

——(1874a), 'Theism', in *Three Essays on Religion*, in J. M. Robson (ed.), *Essays on Ethics, Religion and Society*. Vol. 10 of *Collected Works of John Stuart Mill*. Toronto: University of Toronto Press, 1969, pp. 429–89.

——(1874b), *Three Essays on Religion*, in J. M. Robson (ed.), *Essays on Ethics, Religion and Society*. Vol. 10 of *Collected Works of John Stuart Mill*. Toronto: University of Toronto Press, 1969, pp. 369–489.

——(1874c), 'Utility of religion', in *Three Essays on Religion*, in J. M. Robson (ed.), *Essays on Ethics, Religion and Society*. Vol. 10 of *Collected Works of John Stuart Mill*. Toronto: University of Toronto Press, 1969, pp. 403–28.

Moore, G. E. (1903), *Principia Ethica*. London and New York: Cambridge University Press, 1959.

Packe, Michael St. John (1954), *The Life of John Stuart Mill*. London: Secker and Warburg.

Plato (1937), 'Protagoras', in B. Jowett (trans.), *The Dialogues of Plato* (first published 1892). New York: Random House, pp. 81–130.

Rawls, John (1955), 'Two concepts of rules'. *The Philosophical Review* 64, 3–32.

——(1971), *A Theory of Justice*. Cambridge, MA: Harvard University Press.

Ross, W. D. (1930), *The Right and the Good*. Oxford: Clarendon Press.

Rousseau, Jean-Jacques (1762), *On the Social Contract*. New York: St Martin's Press, 1978.

Schneewind, J. B. (1976), 'Concerning some criticisms of Mill's *Utilitarianism*, 1861–76', in John M. Robson and Michael Laine (eds), *James and John Stuart Mill: Papers of the Centenary Conference*. Toronto and Buffalo: University of Toronto Press, pp. 35–54.

——(ed.) (1965), *Mill's Ethical Writings*. London: Collier-Macmillan; New York: Collier Books.

Sidgwick, Henry (1874; 7th edn, 1907), *Methods of Ethics*. London: Macmillan, 1967.

Urmson, J. O. (1953), 'The interpretation of the philosophy of J. S. Mill'. *Philosophical Quarterly* 3, 33–40.

INDEX

a priori theory 24, 33
affirmative action 95, 97
altruism 42
An Examination of Sir William Hamilton's Philosophy 17
Analysis of the Phenomena of the Human Mind 75
animal suffering 53
appetites, animal 48
Aristotle 13, 86, 87, 130
art, practical 30, 31
association, associationism 75, 76, 81, 86
Auguste Comte and Positivism 17, 42
Autobiography 13, 17

Bacon, Francis 15
'Bentham' 15
Bentham, Jeremy 1, 2, 9, 13, 14, 18–22, 24–5, 38, 43, 70, 71, 75, 94, 108, 125, 126
Benthamite 67
Birks, T. R. 126
birth control 37, 55, 61
blame, blamable, blameworthiness, blameworthy 25, 42, 100
Bradley, F. H. 126–8
Brandt, Richard 129

Calderwood 126
Carritt, E. F. 129
categorical imperative 34, 108
causation, contributory 63
character 51, 60, 61, 70, 76, 109
Christian, Christianity 61, 127
civilization 63, 69, 73, 76, 124
'Coleridge' 15
Collected Works of John Stuart Mill 30
competent judges 50, 67, 68
Comte, Auguste 15, 62, 74
conscience 25, 51, 67, 69, 70, 72, 73, 76, 98, 99
consequences 7–10, 21, 24, 25, 29, 35, 38, 39, 48, 59, 60, 62, 64, 66, 70, 71, 77, 82, 93, 104, 110, 112
  accidental vs. natural 41
  actual 11
  foreseeable 11, 12, 41
consequentialism, consequentialist 3–5, 128, 130
Considerations on Representative Government 16, 112
contentment 45
cooperation 76, 77

Darwin 86
death penalty 92

degree, difference of, vs difference of kind 106
deontological, deontologists 4–6
deserve, deserved, desert 94, 95, 104, 116, 118, 121–3
desirable 37, 42, 78–89, 99, 127
 analogy to visible and audible 78, 126
desire, as proof of desirable 37, 77–89
dignity, sense of 45, 46
dilemmas, moral 34
disobedience, civil 92, 93
divine command theory 8, 22, 35, 38, 86, 105
duty, duties 4–6, 42, 57–60, 67, 71, 73, 76, 90, 95, 98, 100, 116, 121, 129
 of charity 100
 perfect and imperfect 100, 101

East India Company 14
education 55, 57, 68–70, 73, 74, 96, 109, 119
empirical 36
empirical theory 24
empiricism 15
environmental ethics 52
Epicurus 39, 40
equality, inequality 76, 77, 96, 113–16, 118, 119, 121
 of condition 96
 of opportunity 96
Ethical and Political Thinking 129
Ethical Studies 126
'Ethics in America' 130
euthanasia 65, 66
expedient, expediency 39, 40, 42, 62, 63, 68, 96, 98, 99, 104, 106, 116, 118, 121, 123
 idea of 102

fairness 115

fallacy
 naturalistic 128
 of composition 78
family planning, *see* birth control
feelings, moral 73
 innate or acquired 73, 76
 natural 73
 social 73
felicific calculus 20
feminists 15
Fraser's Magazine 14, 17, 125
freedom, *see* liberty
Fundamental Principles of the Metaphysics of Morals 130

God, Deity, Ruler of the Universe 6–8, 17, 24, 35, 36, 61, 70, 71, 73
godless doctrine 39, 61, 68, 123
Grote, John 126

habit, habitual 75, 82, 86, 87
Handbook of Moral Philosophy 125
happiness, unhappiness 1, 3–5, 7, 9, 15, 18, 24, 25, 28, 31, 32, 40–3, 45, 50–6, 64, 66–9, 71, 72, 74–80, 83–5, 88, 91, 106, 118, 124, 126, 127
happiness, parts of 37, 77, 80–2, 84, 86–8
harm 102
hedonic calculus 20
hedonism, hedonist 9, 10, 24, 27, 30, 39, 45, 46, 49, 51, 68, 87, 88, 126–8, 130
 ethical 20
 psychological 20, 21, 86
Hegel 108, 113
History of European Morals 125
Hobbes, Thomas 106, 111, 117
honesty, truthfulness, veracity 5, 62–4
Hume, David 16

immigrants 105
impartial, partial, impartiality,
    partiality 95, 97, 116, 121
imperatives 31
inductive theory 24, 33
inequality, *see* equality
inheritance 96, 97
injustice, *see* just, justice
instincts, instinctive 91, 105
intention vs. motive 59, 60
*Introduction to the Principles of
    Morals and Legislation* 13, 19,
    125
introspection 113 *see also*
    psychology, introspective
intuit, intuitionism, intuitionist,
    intuitive 6, 7, 19, 22–4, 33, 35,
    72, 73, 86, 107, 114, 117, 122,
    127, 128
Jesus 57, 61
just, unjust, justice, injustice 23, 24,
    26–8, 89–121
acts vs states of affairs 121, 122
as rule of action 23, 26
concept, idea, notion of 89, 91,
    98, 102, 104, 109, 110, 120
distributive 89, 113, 114
in punishment 90
of wages and taxation 90, 113,
    114
of wealth and income 89, 113
penal 89, 113
retributive 89
sense of 97
sentiment, feeling of 23, 26, 28,
    89–91, 98, 102, 104, 112, 113,
    118, 119, 121–3, 130

Kant, Immanuel 34, 35, 103, 104,
    108, 129

law 98
Lecky, W. E. H. 125, 127

Leviathan 106
liberty, liberties, freedom 104,
    115–17
life, art or theory of 25, 41, 42, 82,
    85, 99
Locke, John 15–16
love 87
lying, *see* honesty

Marx 16, 54
maximizing, maximized,
    maximization, maximum 41,
    57, 64, 99, 115, 129
mental 'crisis' 14
meritorious 42, 129
metaphysical 83
Methods of Ethics 126
Mill, Harriet Taylor 16 *see also*
    Taylor, Harriet
Mill, James 13, 14, 18, 75
Mill's Ethical Writings 129
Mill's life 12–18
Modern Utilitarianism 126
Moore, G. E. 128
*Moral Philosophy: Classic Texts
    and Contemporary Problems*
    130
moral reason 7
moral sense 6, 7, 13, 19, 24, 32, 35,
    38
morality, progressive 33, 35, 38
Morley, John 125, 127
motive, motives, motivation 25,
    57–9, 68, 69, 72, 75, 76, 86, 111

nature, natural law, law of nature 4,
    6, 8, 13, 17, 19, 22, 24, 61, 91,
    112
nature, state of 106, 107
necessity, doctrine of 110
Nicomachean Ethics 86, 130
Novalis 53

On Liberty 12, 15, 16, 50
On the Social Contract 111
overpopulation 36
Owen, Robert 109, 110, 112

pacifism 94
pain, *see* pleasure
Paley, William 125, 126
Parliament 17, 55
particularism 32
paternalism, paternalistic 109
patriotism 4
peace 117
persons, distinction between 116
Plato 30
pleasure, pain 8, 10, 19–22, 24, 25,
    29, 38–56, 64–8, 70, 71, 73, 75,
    76, 80–7, 108, 120, 128
  animal vs intellectual 44
  first-order vs second-order 44, 46
  higher and lower 41–50, 55, 126,
    128
  intensity and duration 20, 43, 67
  net 21
  quality, quantity of 20, 22, 24, 27,
    38, 42–52, 67, 68, 88, 123,
    127
  quantity of, *see* quality of
pleasure machine 51
poverty 96, 116
praiseworthy 100 *see also* blame,
    blameworthy
preference 43, 52, 83, 111, 123
Principia Ethica 128
Principles of Political Economy 12,
    15, 16, 125
progress, moral and social 37, 66,
    68, 77
promise, promises 94, 95, 118
proof 19, 26, 28, 29, 37, 77–89, 126,
    129
Protagoras 29
Providence 61, 74

psychology, psychological 77, 82,
    83, 85–8, 109, 124
  associationist 75, 80
  introspective 46, 47
punishment 25, 26, 42, 61, 71, 98,
    99, 102, 107–11, 117, 118, 121
  capital 94 *see also* death penalty
  degree of 113
  deterrent 26, 92, 94, 107, 108, 112
  reformative 26, 94
  retributive 94, 108, 112, 113, 122
  therapeutic 109

Rashdall, Hastings 128
rational action 12
Rawls, John 115, 116, 129
realism, moral 31, 32
religion, religions, religious 4, 7, 8,
    17, 61, 72, 74, 76
religion of humanity 15, 17, 62
right
  by conquest 107
  correlative to duty 100, 101, 117,
    121
  legal 92, 121
  moral 92, 121
  natural 37, 105
  to equality 116, 119
  to liberty
Right and the Good, The 129
rights, rights theorists 5, 6, 22, 24,
    27, 67, 104, 105, 107, 115, 117,
    119, 123, 129
  property 104, 120
Ross, W. D. 129
Rousseau 111
rule, rules 31, 32, 52, 62–7, 69, 72,
    99, 103, 104, 123, 124, 126, 128,
    129
sacrifice 57
sanctions 22, 25, 27, 61, 68–77, 104,
    119, 124
  external 22, 25, 69, 70, 73, 75, 76

internal 22, 25, 69, 70, 71, 72, 75
moral 22
penal 90, 98, 121
political 22, 70
popular 22, 70
religious 22, 70
ultimate 25, 69, 72, 74–6

Sartre, Jean Paul 34
Schneewind, J. B. 125–7
science 30, 31
secondary principle 40, 67, 126
security 5, 26, 90, 102, 106, 107, 117, 123
'Sedgwick's Discourse' 41
self-defence 102, 109, 110
self-observation 82, 85, 123
sentiments, moral 75 see also feelings, moral
Sidgwick, Henry 9, 126–8
slaves, slavery 118, 119
social contract 4, 5, 105, 111, 112, 122
socialism 16, 54, 55
Socrates 29, 30, 45
Stephen, Fitzjames 125
Stoics 60
Subjection of Women, The 17, 37, 55
suicide 53
swine, doctrine worthy of 23, 26, 39, 43, 45, 49, 123
supererogation 42
sympathy 56, 60, 72, 75, 90, 102, 122
System of Logic 12, 15, 17, 31, 40, 42, 125

taxation 26
Taylor, Harriet 15 see also Mill, Harriet Taylor
Taylor, Mr. 65
teleological 4

tend, tendency 12, 18, 32, 40, 69
'The Utility of Religion' 17
'Theism' 17
Theory of Justice, A 115, 129
Theory of Good and Evil, The 128
Three Essays on Religion 17
Traite/ de Legislation 13
truth 62
truths, moral 31
tyranny of the majority 16

unhappiness, see happiness
universalizability 104
Urmson, J. O. 129
utilitarianism, utilitarian
act- 10–12, 25, 38, 40, 60, 63–7, 99, 129
direct 10, 11
ideal 9, 128
indirect 10, 11
rule- 11, 25, 38, 40, 60, 63–4, 66, 68, 99, 129
utility
diminishing marginal 116
expected 115, 116
'Utility of Religion' 62

value
expected 21
instrumental 5, 21, 48, 53
intrinsic 6, 10, 48, 53, 83, 84, 87, 89, 124
veracity, see honesty
virtue, virtuous 57, 61, 63, 71, 81, 83, 86, 126, 128
virtue ethics 4–6, 59

war 93
will 83, 84, 111
free 110–11
women's suffrage 17
Wordsworth 15
worthiness 99